What could be a better tribute to Eric Sevareid than that these two delightful, adventuresome, and modest young men undertook to re-create the great broadcaster's adolescent canoe trip from Minneapolis to Hudson Bay? As you are swept along with Colton and Sean in *Adventure North,* you can't help liking these two remarkable young men as they pursue what will surely be the most important rite of passage in their lives. Now, if they use what they have learned in young manhood as wisely as did Sevareid, they might just change the world.

- Clay Jenkinson, Author of *The Character of Meriwether Lewis: Explorer in the Wilderness*, Bismarck, North Dakota

Adventure North fits the bill as a lively, entertaining and stirring account of teenage exploits in the natural world rarely sought out for, much less experienced, by today's youth.

In truth, however, it is an inspirational narrative for all ages on personal growth through pushing past one's comfort zone, reliance on others, and most importantly, friendship. While the title indicates the route taken by the pair, it easily symbolizes the upwardly character development that results.

- Charles Friedbauer, Outdoors Reporter, Writer, Chaska, Minnesota

Adventure North

by

Sean Bloomfield

Adventure North

For more information and copies of this book, visit www.hudsonbaybook.com

To Colton…
For adventure's reflection means less when
experienced alone.

Table of Contents

Foreword by Colton Witte

Adventure North is a story like no other. At eighteen, in the 21st century, the last thing Sean and I should have been thinking about was dreamy disconnection. Kids are often taught to be pragmatic, social, and within reach one hundred percent of the time. Sean and I, however, chose quite the opposite path.

For as long as I can remember, he and I dreamed of going on a grand journey, for no other reason than the journey itself. To us, there is something poetic and exhilarating about the experiences between the start and end of a path, regardless of the destination. This has always been our mindset. Wanderers and explorers; that is who we have always been.

Dreaming was a way for us to season an otherwise relatively predictable world to our wilder tastes. It was mere coincidence that our dreams led us to leave society and its comforts. We are both people persons; we didn't aim to be recluses. Neither did we hate technology; we just saw the value of temporarily escaping it.

But in so doing, we learned lessons that cannot be learned elsewhere. Without the encumbrance of practicality, we learned that any dream can be accomplished with simple analysis, planning, and execution. Without technology and society, we learned the crucial importance of introspection.

I hope that these lessons are what you take away from reading *Adventure North*. Venture outside your comfort zone, whether that is into the wilds of nature or the dynamics of people and culture. It doesn't matter where or how. It's the activity, rather than the destination, that teaches. While you're doing so, think critically about yourself and your place in the world around you. Perhaps most importantly, go out and live with intention.

Preface

On April 28, 2008, Colton Witte, a neighborhood friend, and I pushed our canoe into the Minnesota River in downtown Chaska, a suburb of Minneapolis. Our destination was 2,200 miles to the north, at York Factory on the Hudson Bay, within the permafrost reaches of the North Atlantic Ocean in Manitoba, Canada. The two of us had accelerated our studies and graduated high school five weeks before departure. The idea came from a book my father passed down to me in seventh grade, *Canoeing with the Cree*. It is the story of two high school graduates from Minneapolis, Eric Sevareid and Walter Port, who embarked on the same adventure in 1930. I read it, showed it to my friend Colton, and somewhere along the line we decided that we would do it. In reading the book, we concentrated on the adventure and ignored the miseries, and for that I am grateful. If we hadn't ignored them, we likely wouldn't have embarked on such an undertaking.

Canoeing to Hudson Bay was, and remains, a contradiction. It was the adventure of a lifetime, and two of the most challenging months of my life. If I could go back in time, knowing what I know now, I would do it in a heartbeat – but I would never do it again today. Even during the trip, there were many moments when I felt both unsatisfied and content, or both miserable and joyous, all at once. Each night contained a triumphant tone of accomplishment, while every morning was met with a depressed sense of enslavement. We felt obligated and inspired to continue on, especially when the going got tough. Throughout this book, I attempt to convey those feelings as accurately as possible. What results is not always the most romantic portrayal of the wilderness, but neither is real life in the woods.

To my paddling partner and best friend, Colton, I owe my life. Words cannot describe my gratitude, and without him, the trip would never have happened. Throughout the forty-nine days that we spent together on this voyage, Colton went through more pain and agony than many can imagine. The fact that he continued on in such trying times shows more bravery than I have ever encountered from another human, and for that I am forever thankful. He pushed me in my trying times, just as any superb team member does. I would not have replaced him with the best canoeist in the world.

Finally, I would like to thank our parents for allowing us, two overconfident teenagers, to venture into the unknown and live out a dream. Colton's parents, Dan and Kathy, along with my parents, Patrick and Patricia, deserve a medal for their support. In fact, my father went so far as to donate his North Bay canoe to the journey. As a father now, I can finally begin to understand the mental turmoil they must have gone through in the weeks while we were away. It hadn't occurred to us just how frightening it was to let go and *hope* that all would go as planned. My deepest wish is that someday I will be just as courageous a parent as they were, even if my children grow up to be half as reckless as Colton and I.

This story is an account of the amazing adventure that the two of us embarked on at just eighteen years old. Through strong currents, sub-freezing temperatures, fierce headwinds, raging rapids, poor health, and more misery than I can begin to describe, we found something that most Americans think is gone: a true adventure. And we had a heck of a time doing it.

Adventure North

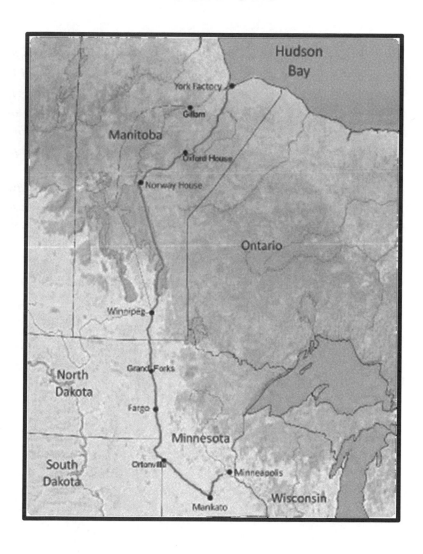

"They got in, took up their paddles, and pushed off, heading against the flow, up the Minnesota 300 miles to Ortonville and Big Stone Lake. That should take two weeks, they figure. After that, it's down the north-flowing Red River, across Lake Winnipeg the long way, and then to the Hayes River and 16 sets of rapids down to Hudson Bay, carrying bear spray against the chance of polar bears.

Just a jaunt of 2,250 miles or so. Then back to Chaska in time for the State Fair and a chance to rekindle a high school romance or two. Sean will attend Minnesota State, Mankato, in the fall. Colton hasn't picked a college yet.

They pushed out into the swollen, brown river.

'Take a right!' yelled Colton's dad, Dan.

Right was the right way – up stream, up the continent, up to Hudson Bay."

-Nick Coleman

Columnist - *Minneapolis Star Tribune*

April 29, 2008.

CHAPTER 1

Dreams

Day 46 - June 12, 2008 – Southwest corner of Swampy Lake in Manitoba

The alarm rang with unnerving normalcy. It was far too early in the morning. My slumber had begun what felt like only minutes prior. This feeling, too, had become normal. I poked my head out of the sleeping bag to investigate the source of the ear-shattering buzz. A battery-powered clock was lying directly above my head at the wall of the tent.

"4:30 A.M." flashed mockingly in the florescent backlight. The light was totally unnecessary. Days away from the Summer Solstice and just beyond one hundred sixty miles southwest of Hudson Bay, Manitoba, so far north that polar bears outnumber people, it would have been difficult to find darkness had we wanted to.

Below the time was a small thermometer. Inside our tent, the temperature was registering in at a frosty twenty-five degrees Fahrenheit. It seemed impossible that it was June. At six feet tall and one hundred forty pounds, I was as lanky as they come, and throughout the eighteen years of my life, cold never mixed well with lankiness. This morning was not the first of our trip that I wished for several extra pounds of insulation.

My head turned and I peeked at the door to our tent. It was unrecognizable. Mosquitos, in quantities that I had once thought to be impossible, masked the screen door, waiting for the one barrier standing between them and their prey to be removed. Their thirst was understandable; less than a dozen people travel through this area each year, and human blood was a valuable commodity. We were their Thanksgiving feast.

From my sleeping bag, after my head came both hands. I gingerly removed them to inspect the damage from two days prior. Aside from the many blisters, they were visually fine. That stood opposite from the way they felt, as if on fire, every skin cell scalded by the most severe burn imaginable, caused simply by a mistaken coating of oil via our can of bear repellant. It made sense now what the rangers had told us – that bear spray could be more useful than a gun against polar bears. To be honest, if I had to pick between getting shot in the leg or sprayed with bear mace again, I would strongly consider the former.

"Alright, that's enough out of you," I finally groaned, tapping the button on the right side of our clock and bringing the obnoxious buzz to a halt.

Less than one foot to my left, always to my left, lay my paddling partner, Colton Witte. Unsurprisingly, his head had yet to surface from his sleeping bag. I was always the first to rise and accepted my responsibility of waking Colton dutifully.

"Colton, get up," I said, shoving his bag with more force than necessary. Without explanation, my wake-up calls had grown in aggression as our trip progressed. Despite this, or perhaps because of it, Colton had made a habit of simply groaning and rolling over.

Giving up for the moment, I crawled out of my bag and to the door. In one swift movement, I slapped the screen to give the mosquitos a momentary shock with one hand, unzipped the door with the other, and rolled outside onto the damp soil. Only several days prior, I would have frantically escaped the swarm of bugs that were now happily making my blood the breakfast of a lifetime. Mosquito bites were the least of my concern though, and my obligatory screen-slap before opening the tent-door was the most defense I was willing to exert.

Standing up, I reached into the pocket of my raincoat for the white woolen winter hat, which was now a mainstay for the cold mornings of our expedition. Pulling it over my thick, shaggy black hair, I thought back to the day on the Red River when I had lost my first hat. Fortunately, my parents were able to bring along another one for our re-supply in Winnipeg, but I shuddered at the thought of losing a hat up here.

Though it was technically light outside, the sun was nowhere to be found. Roughly twenty feet of knee-high grass sloped its way from our tent, beneath a layer of morning frost and down to the lazy Hayes River. Resting above the water was a still, windless fog. Across the river, the land was relatively bare, having recently fallen victim to a forest fire. We were just on the edge of the fire's reach, so several trees remained upright amidst the rubble of their fallen comrades. As I made my way to the water, my boots crunching in the stiff grass, I remarked at the eerie sensation that the fog had draped over our morning. Perhaps it was a calm before the storm ahead.

At the riverbank, I knelt down and soaked my hands in the frigid water. We heard from a group of fishermen on Knee Lake a couple of days prior that less than two weeks ago, pickup trucks were driving on the lake's ice. While scooping the water with my palms and splashing it into my face (the closest thing to a shower in nearly a month), I wondered how long a person could survive if they swamped their canoe in these conditions.

Best not to think about it.

Breakfast was a quick, in-the-tent ordeal after Colton finally awoke, and then we were on our way. The mosquitos continued to swarm our heads and attack our eyes as we loaded the canoe and pushed off into the idle river. It regularly took several minutes for the herd of "skeeters" to lose our scent and trail off. No doubt, due to a lack of bathing, we could surely be smelled from miles away.

Just beyond our campsite, the Hayes flowed into Swampy Lake, which the two of us crossed in silent anticipation. At the far eastern end of the lake would be the start of what we called the "rapids section," forty miles of nearly constant rapids or falls, after which we would be home free – in theory. Here, our white-water paddling would be put to the test, and after a shaky outing the evening before, I will not deny that I was at least slightly nervous.

It was Colton's turn this morning to captain the canoe from the back, or stern. On a normal day, this meant little more than a change of scenery and slightly less legroom. Being several inches shorter, legroom mattered less to Colton than it did to me. Leading into a day full of raging rapids, though, meant he would have to be on the top of his game. The stern position was responsible for steering, and to be in control of the canoe in rapids was to be in control of our lives.

On an island at the eastern end of Swampy Lake, we took refuge from a blistering wind and steadily increasing drizzle. Here we changed out of our dry, pleasant hiking boots, and into our cold, moist neoprene boots. Normally meant for scuba diving, neoprene boots are naturally more at home in the water than your typical footwear. They provide better traction when submerged, continue to offer some small amount of insulation while wet, and they don't retain nearly as much water. As such, dive boots worked quite well for lining, or dragging our canoe through rapids, and kept our regular hiking boots dry. Dry feet is as essential a commodity towards survival as food.

While rounding a bend at the entrance to the river, I looked longingly back at the whitecap-filled Swampy Lake. Wind is perhaps the most frustrating force of nature to a canoeist, but what was ahead for the next two days would be the greatest challenge of our lives. The immediate dangers of running rapids are obvious. Canoeists could, for instance, tip their canoe and fall out, subsequently hitting their heads on rocks, or become pinned beneath fallen branches… so on and so forth.

What was even more worrisome, however, was imagining the aftermath from tipping our canoe. We would almost surely be missing important bits of gear. If we were to lose our tent or stove, any hope of moderate comfort during the remaining journey would be killed. If we were to lose our food pack, we would have an immediate emergency on our hands. Lost paddles or a wrecked canoe… I didn't want to think about what being stranded in these conditions would be like.

Beyond the plan-of-action type problems that would arise from tipping or wrecking, we would also certainly be risking hypothermia in the near freezing downpour. If all went according to plan, the cold and wetness that so tortured us would be limited to our extremities. Falling in, though, would wet our bodies to the core, resulting in possibly unrecoverable disaster.

I swallowed nervously and looked briefly at Colton. His sandy brown hair, normally a short buzz, had grown long and untidy. The headwind blew icy rain onto his exposed head... a final straw.

"Hold on," he called, setting his paddle down in frustration. "I gotta bundle up some more." On went the black and grey hat that had become such a common accessory to Colton's wardrobe. He then pulled the hood of his orange rain jacket over the hat and zipped it up so snug that only his eyes were visible.

"Can you see?" I asked, knowing that his vision would be vital to our success.

After he nodded in the affirmative and returned his paddle to the water, I turned my head forward towards the open, seemingly innocent river ahead of me. One thing that Colton and I noticed was that the person in the bow (me at the time) always seemed to be more anxious while running rapids than the man in the stern. The bow yielded far less control of the craft. You never truly trust a friend, we found, until they've had your life in their hands.

"Ready?" asked Colton.

Do I have a choice? I thought, somewhat sarcastically. I paused for a moment and stared forward towards our eventual goal, one hundred sixty miles ahead: Hudson Bay. "Yep," I said. "Let's do this."

Three months earlier

A vertical strip of light glimmered off the spotted carpet floor of Ms. Flom's second floor classroom. Her windows pointed to the east, and the rising March sun shone through the cracks in the blinds, adding a frosty glare to the otherwise dimly lit room. The projector hanging from the ceiling shot the image of a map onto a whiteboard. Thirty sophomores stared sleepily at me as I stood in the front of the room, wondering who the shaggy senior before them was and why he was showing a map that combined Minnesota and central Canada.

"Sean, why don't you describe your trip to the class?" said Ms. Flom, who was standing by the door with an encouraging smile.

"Sure," I said, pointing a yardstick to the map projection. "We're starting out here in Chaska, April 28th this year, on the Minnesota River, and then paddling up that for about three or four hundred miles." I looked back out to the class to gauge their interest. A couple faces I knew well from sports, or as the younger siblings of friends, but most were strangers to me. Each grade of Chaska High School held near seven hundred students, so it was a rare sighting to find an underclassman with whom I was on a first-name basis; perhaps it was the first period lull, but the looks on their faces suggested they cared little to change that. One boy's eyes flickered and I noticed his head twitch, like he had just awoken abruptly from a dream in which he was falling.

"From the headwaters of the Minnesota River," I continued, "we'll hook in with the Red River over on the Minnesota-North Dakota border. The Red flows north into Canada, eventually flowing into Lake Winnipeg."

I pointed to a massive blue blob on the map, just north of the Canadian border. A few of the tenth graders perked up when they saw the big lake.

"It's the eleventh biggest lake in the world, but surprisingly shallow. The average depth is under forty feet. . ." I looked back to my audience. I was losing them. A rookie mistake to get into the gritty details. They wanted adventure.

"After Lake Winnipeg, we'll connect with the Hayes River, which flows through a series of rapids, rivers, and lakes all the way to Hudson Bay." I flashed a satisfied grin, almost like I had already completed the trek. The class looked uninspired. It was time for my trump card. "The area around Hudson Bay has one of the highest concentrations of polar bears in the world." If I had any muscles on my arms, this was where I would have flexed them.

"Oh, polar bears are so cute!" a group of girls in the front piped up. Hardly the impressed reaction I was hoping for.

The tenth grade English class I was presenting to had just finished reading *Into the Wild* by Jon Krakauer, a classic true story of a young man who, upon graduating from college, gave up his money and possessions to live in the wild. Two years later, he was found dead in the Alaskan bush (hardly a spoiler, as this fact is made clear on the book's first page). The story has inspired scores of adventurers, both wise and not, to live their dreams of wilderness escape. We hoped we would go down as the former.

Our own story started out for the same simple reason: adventure. Since the dawn of man, humans have craved adventure – its wonder, its imagination, and its absolute freedom. Adventure may come in a variety of shapes and sizes, but ours was one that Minnesotans in particular have shared for decades. It included a search for a simpler life, one where the imagination of what lies around the next bend captures you, and where we could truly find ourselves at the core of human existence. There is nothing easy about surviving in nature, yet the concept holds such allure for generations young and old. Perhaps the human mind has not yet adapted to the confines of city-life, where technology and modern comforts provide us with more than our ancient ancestors could have cared to hope for. Maybe we have tied adventure to escape, and our need to escape the rituals of life in the 21st century pushes us out that front door and into the unknown, where the security of knowing what lies ahead is left behind.

Our thirst for adventure stemmed not from *Into the Wild*, but *Canoeing with the Cree*. It is the story in which Eric Sevareid chronicled his journey along the same route as ours. Many remember Sevareid from his subsequent award-winning journalism career, most notably at CBS. The book follows two Minneapolis teens, Sevareid and his friend Walter Port, fresh out of high school in 1930, who paddle a canoe from their hometown to York Factory at Hudson Bay in northern Manitoba.

"Why are you guys doing this?" piped up a boy in the back. He asked the question as though I couldn't convince him to take our trip for a million dollars.

"For fun." I shrugged. Some people only seemed to see the misery of our journey.

"I think it sounds sweet!" A few boys finally woke up and began to whisper their own summer adventures to each other. These were my kind of sophomores. My experience was that, in fact, most who heard of our voyage envied us. Kids our age and younger discussed their camping trips, while adults reminisced of their ambitious outings from a past life.

Minnesotans have a special love for the outdoors, one that has been steeped into their culture and bloodlines for generations. Unfortunately, urbanization lies in the way. The love is still there, but the resources for children to build log cabins in the woods or to go on hikes through seemingly uncharted land just outside their backyards are quickly dwindling. Perhaps that was why we chose our route; the Minnesota River flowed right through our growing suburban town, and while the river bordered civilization, it connected to virtually uncharted territory beyond our imaginations. That we would be forced to escape civilization by paddling the river upstream was harshly symbolic.

For many Minnesotans, dreams of the outdoors can be partially fulfilled by venturing into the Boundary Waters Canoe Area (BWCA) on the border of Minnesota and Ontario. It is a home away from home for many outdoorsmen... a Minnesota holy-land for anglers, canoeists, campers, and anyone else who lives for the beauty of untouched wilderness. Here, in the Boundary Waters, was where I was introduced to canoeing at the ripe age of seven. Naturally, I did little more than dip my toy paddle into the water from the middle of the canoe, while my parents did the real grunt work, but I caught the paddling bug nonetheless.

It wasn't until the summer after fourth grade that I was able to share this bug with a fellow dreamer. A neighbor of the previous three years, Colton Witte, and his father joined my father and me, along with Colton's uncle and cousin from Duluth, on a weeklong trip into the heart of the BWCA. From here on out, this group, along with another family or two, would take an annual trip to somewhere in the vast Boundary Waters wilderness. Colton and I were hooked, indeed.

My childhood home in Chaska, Minnesota was in a neighborhood typical of the suburban sprawl that took place across the United States in the late twentieth century. A four-level split wrapped in brown wooden siding, it sat beneath the shade of a massive cottonwood tree and backed up to a small lake. Three houses down the shoreline was Colton's home. After catching the paddling bug in elementary school, the two of us spent our summers around the lake, building forts on shore and using our canoe to explore the chain of lakes connected to ours.

At age twelve, several weeks before reading Eric Sevareid's tale, Colton and I took our first solo canoe trip. It was nothing extraordinary: a one-night excursion away from our parents' camp in the Boundary Waters. We were highly unprepared. Having eaten dinner at the camp with our fathers, all we brought for food were four granola bars and miniature bags of dry cereal for breakfast the next day. The night went well. While staring at our campfire, we listened in awe to a pack of wolves howling on the opposite shore and went to sleep on top of the world.

Morning came with a cold wind blowing from across the lake into our exposed campsite. The wood we had gathered the day before was soaked from an overnight rain, and so after a miserable attempt to create a fire from them failed, we moved on in futility to the previous night's wrappers. Defeated, we hiked into the woods to escape the wind and eat our cereal, cold and uncomfortable. Eventually, we swallowed our pride and paddled back to our parents' camp, making sure to sound like we had conquered the outing with flying colors.

Perhaps the beauty of being twelve is that you soon forget your mishaps and believe that the next time you do something, it will be different, undoubtedly better. For this reason, we were far from deterred and continued to dream. Shortly after returning to Chaska, *Canoeing with the Cree* came into my possession. I was electrified. As soon as I could peel myself from it, I presented the book to Colton. Not long after, we decided, "What the heck? Let's do it!"

"What have you and Colton done to prepare for your adventure?" asked Ms. Flom. "Chris McCandless, many would argue, was woefully unprepared. How have you guys convinced your parents that you will have a different fate?"

I laughed. It had been a long road convincing our poor parents to approve of the trip. Initially, when we were in 7th grade, they kind of chuckled and gave us encouraging smiles. Clearly, their expectations of our impractical dreams weren't high. I can't blame them; Colton and I had a reputation of hatching cockamamie plans. This was around the same time that we were convinced we would be "quintillionaire" business owners who invented high-tech gadgets and invested wiser than anybody else in the world had yet imagined. Our business would be called "Bloomitte Enterprises," a combination of our two last names, and I'm certain we had an entire binder full of plans and sketches.

For several years, canoeing to Hudson Bay remained only a dream, something our friends and family assumed would be lost along with our other childhood ambitions, the way that grandiose desires have a way of doing: ceded to more easily achievable and applicable goals.

Everything changed the summer after ninth grade. We had just finished another annual Boundary Waters trip, and Colton and I were spending a week at his grandparents' house in northern Wisconsin. Here, we happened to be near the headwaters of the St. Croix River. A simple drive to the river was all that it took. Colton looked at it and said, "You know, this river flows all the way down to the Mississippi River back by home. We should paddle down it, just the two of us, in preparation for the Hudson Bay trip."

I laughed at the idea on first thought, just as others had previously laughed at our plans. But after thinking about it for a moment, I realized that there was really no reason we could not do it. We were a mere three years away from when we planned on doing the Hudson Bay trip and we still had yet to prove ourselves in the wild. Hudson Bay would be over two thousand miles of adventure. After some research, we found that the St. Croix River, which for a majority of its course defines the border between Minnesota and Wisconsin, was about one hundred forty miles long. It became obvious that if we had a chance at surviving the Hudson Bay trip, let alone finishing, we had to begin preparing with trips of this sort.

"Two years ago, we canoed down the St. Croix River, which took us six days," I said to the class. "And then last summer, we paddled from Lake of the Woods to Lake Superior, along the Canadian border. That was about four hundred fifty miles and took twelve days. We've really just been able to convince our parents by succeeding on our practice trips.

"Would you guys like to see some pictures from the last trip?" I had forty-five minutes slotted to speak and had only used five. My question was risky, for a big part of me assumed they would say no. To my fortune, they were good sports and nodded along pleasantly the rest of the time. As I bade the class farewell, I was sure that I heard a few remarks about their desire for us to come back alive. A cheerful thought!

The remainder of our senior year came and went quickly. We accelerated our studies and graduated later that month upon the conclusion of third quarter. That gave us time to prepare for an April 28th departure. Everything went off without a hitch, except for a senior prank we childishly decided to pull on our last day of school by dropping crickets from a balcony over the school commons. After a long talk with the school-assigned police officer and administrators, we each received two-hundred-fifty-dollar fines for Public Nuisance and an hour of community service, which we dutifully completed by cleaning the grounds of Chaska High School.

One thing did come unexpectedly in the week leading up to our departure – publicity. We had previously attempted to garner media attention by contacting several newspapers along the way, some of the Twin Cities' news stations, as well as local and national sporting goods stores for sponsorship. Silence was our only response, but that did little to bother us. We even convinced ourselves that it was better this way; the last thing we wanted to be was "corporate sellouts."

Only days before setting off, two local news channels received word of our trip and recorded special segments about us. Then two days before we left, a Minneapolis *Star Tribune* columnist named Nick Coleman wrote a piece on Eric Sevareid, detailing how he had been inspiring Minnesotan adventurers for years. He had not yet heard of us. My father read the article and emailed Mr. Coleman right away to inform him of our trip. Upon learning of it, Nick was nearly as excited about the adventure as Colton and I.

Sunday, April 27th arrived too quickly. Exhausted from a long night spent cherishing our final moments with friends at our senior prom, Colton and I found ourselves with far too much to do in one day. We picked up several last-minute supplies from a nearby outdoors store and squeezed in time to spend with our friends and families. It was amazing how we could be lounging so luxuriously one day, knowing full well what was ahead of us the next.

We spent that evening with our friends and went to bed early. I remember while trying to fall asleep, thinking how quickly the next day had come upon us. For almost as long as we could remember, canoeing to Hudson Bay had been a dream of ours, and when a dream comes true, it's oftentimes difficult to believe, yet here it was. My stomach turned over itself at the realization that this would be my last real bed in some time. Closing my eyes, I smiled in nervous excitement.

CHAPTER 2

Hudson Bay or Bust

The sun rose quicker than expected on the morning of April 28th, and my heart already pounded in anticipation of the task at hand. I hadn't slept well overnight, my mind racing despite the knowledge that sleep would be vital. No matter, I was ready to go.

Up a half-flight of stairs in the kitchen, I attempted to eat a bowl of cereal for breakfast. It wasn't happening. Pushing the soggy cereal bits in circles around the bowl with my spoon, I said under my breath, "Get real; you know you're going to kill for this in four hours. Just eat it!" Not a thing. I never had been good at combining nerves and appetite.

I peered out the sliding glass door through the leafless cottonwood to the lake behind. A miniature breeze rippled across the surface and my heart skipped a beat. We would be on the water in a matter of hours! Exposure to the harsh nature outside would be a small price to pay for the freedom of a summer in the woods.

Beside me sat my two-year-old Black Lab, Cinder, staring up at me with her ears perked. "No begging!" I said instinctively. Then, after a quick glance around to make sure my parents weren't near, I walked over to the drawer with her dog treats and dropped a couple for her on the hardwood kitchen floor. "You're lucky I'm gonna be gone for a couple of months," I said to her seriously. "Otherwise, I never could have risked that."

I wondered if Cinder knew that she would not be seeing me for several months, or in her case, at least three dog-years. Of course she didn't, but that naïve quality is why people love dogs so much. They treat every moment with us as though they are as happy as can be, merely to be in our presence.

Gathering myself, I walked to the closet in our front entryway and pulled my father's heavy rain jacket over my head. He had been gracious enough to lend it to me for the duration of the trip. I tried to ignore the fact that I might never see this place, my home, again. Of course, we knew that there would be little danger for the first several hundred, if not thousand, miles along our course. It would be the end – the land of massive lakes, violent rapids, polar bears, and permafrost – that would be our most obvious pitfall. Rarely did we mention these dangers, except of course when we were trying to impress the girls and our friends at school (neither were usually so convinced).

For a moment, I considered finding my parents upstairs to say goodbye. I didn't hear a lot of noise, so I assumed they were still asleep. They would, of course, be at the bon voyage planned for our departure in an hour's time, so I sided with providing them a few extra minutes of sleep, and walked out the door.

I noticed immediately upon stepping outside that today would be different than we had imagined. The thermometer perched on the exterior wall next to my parents' front door read twenty-eight degrees Fahrenheit. Winter was clinging later than it typically did; it was Monday today, and it had snowed as recently as Friday. Zipping up my rain jacket, it crossed my mind how shockingly light it felt in the brisk spring air. With my hands pushed deep into my pants pockets, I walked the three doors down the street to Colton's home.

Between this moment and when the Witte family moved into our newly developed 1990s neighborhood, during our first grade year, I had made this short hike more times than I would care to imagine. On this particular occasion, though, something seemed different. This time, I would not return home until I had stepped foot on the permafrost banks of Hudson Bay; until we had conquered the North American continent. Or until it had conquered us.

The blue sedan in the Wittes' driveway marked the presence of Colton's girlfriend, Courtney, who sure enough was downstairs with

Colton helping him pack last-minute supplies when I arrived. Most of our gear was filled and ready to go from the night before, with the exception of our custom-made food pack. For a shop project in school, Colton had built an aluminum box that would fit inside our largest pack and which, hopefully, would be waterproof enough to keep our food dry. At least, he had started to build the box. The waterproof seal had just been completed the previous night and would take several days to dry, so our parents would have to drop it off with us a week or two after departure. Until that point, we would keep our food in a cardboard box lined with garbage bags and stuffed inside a pack. We were quite well prepared, indeed.

Other than food, which we had packed only enough to last a week or two, considering we would paddle by towns almost daily on the American half of the route, our supply list began with an eighteen-foot Bell North Bay model canoe and a two-person single-wall tent that we ordered online (by "two-person tent," I mean a "one-person-plus-a-dog tent"). We also brought one sleeping bag each, both rated to maintain warmth down to twenty degrees, a survival bag with first aid supplies, three bent-shaft paddles, a digital camera, one lifejacket each, two small backpacking single-burner stoves, a tank of white gas for the stoves, maps, a compass, a deck of waterproof cards, and a five-gallon jug of water that we would use until Lake Winnipeg, filling up in towns whenever possible to avoid filtering water from the pesticide-packed Minnesota and Red Rivers.

Our lack of a GPS (Global Positioning System) was intentional, as we would do our best to replicate Sevareid and Port's 1930 expedition by limiting our access to modern amenities. GPS technology was not entirely left behind, though – a SPOT Messenger had been given to us as a Christmas gift. It should be noted that this was in essence a gift to our loved ones, for it did little or nothing to assist Colton and me during the course of the trip. The size of a fist, a SPOT Messenger is a device that lacks an actual screen, but instead sports four small buttons. One is an on and off button, and two are used for emergency beacons, depending on the severity of the emergency. The last button, the only one (other than the power button) that Colton or I hoped to ever have to push, shoots off an "all-clear" signal with our GPS coordinates attached on a link to Google Maps, to any email connected to our account. This was a perfect compromise to allow our parents the peace of mind to sleep at night.

We each also brought along our primitive cell phones, though we would keep them off at almost all times, tucked away in our waterproof pack, knowing that reception and charging would be virtually impossible in the wild. There would be two points – one in Montevideo on the Minnesota River, and the other in Winnipeg just to the north of the Canadian border – where our parents planned to meet us for a re-supply and layover. These two days would require some level of communication with the outside world. As much as we hoped to disconnect from technology for the duration of our journey, we knew the phones would serve us well for only the most necessary circumstances.

With the help of Courtney, we threw the gear into my truck, a forest-green '96 S-10, and moved on to loading the canoe into Colton's baby blue '86 Silverado. Just as we were readying to leave, Colton got a flat tire – a perfect start.

Our plan was to push off in downtown Chaska on the Minnesota River, just a few miles from our homes. We were hoping to arrive at the park by 6:45 AM, and it was already nearly 7:00 by the time we realized Colton's tire was flat, so I drove to the park alone in case any well-wishers had already arrived.

Sure enough, several of our friends were there, waiting in the gravel parking lot, along with a camera operator from a local news channel. Only two steps out of the car and the reporter had already confronted me. "Hey, are you either Sean or Colton?" the man asked, his camera resting over his right shoulder. I envied his red winter coat; he looked quite comfortable, considering the temperature.

"Uh yeah," I responded, turning away for a moment to reach through the open window of my truck to the center console. "I'm Sean. What's up?"

"Where's the partner?"

"Oh, he got a flat tire." I laughed. My body was now halfway inside the truck and my feet off the ground. The thought crossed my mind how ludicrous this must look, and I then realized that it would have been easier to simply open the truck door. "He'll be here in a few minutes," I called.

"Need a hand?" asked the reporter finally. Of course, just as he asked, I found what I had been looking for: a solid black winter hat that I kept in the car for emergencies. Since I had forgotten my preferred hat at home, this absolutely qualified as an emergency.

"Nope, found it!" I exclaimed, jumping backwards out of the driver door window and firmly back onto the gravel.

The reporter seemed uninterested. "Mind if I get an interview?"

"Yeah, no problem."

The cameraman threaded a microphone under my jacket and up to the collar of my undershirt. He aimed the camera at me and asked a few questions. Everything felt so glamorous. In the background, I could see several of my friends making faces at me.

As the minutes passed, additional well-wishers began to arrive, along with several more reporters, including the *Star Tribune* columnist, Mr. Coleman. Small snowflakes mixed with sleet began to fall over our shoulders. The weather seemed to be debating just how miserable it could make us on our first day. Everybody, myself included, was wondering where Colton was. I answered more questions from reporters but didn't want to do too much at the moment without Colton accompanying me. We were a team.

Just when I began to grow genuinely worried, Colton's Chevy crested the hill that overlooked the park and rumbled down into the parking lot with our much-needed canoe. A sarcastic cheer, started by me, ensued.

The goodbyes were long and emotional, some so emotional that they had to be split up by an occasional interview or going-away gift from friends. We took pictures with family by the water, next to the lifeless shrubs that had yet to sprout buds. In my head, for some reason, I had always imagined it to be warm and green on the day of our departure. Instead, we were surrounded by a sea of lifeless brown and grey.

At last it was time – the moment we had been waiting for. It seemed as though the last six years of our lives had been leading up to one single event, and this was it. I couldn't say how many times I played this image in my head, and the fact that it was actually happening seemed surreal.

Colton and I dueled in a complicated hands game that our group of friends had made up, similar to "rock-paper-scissors," to see who would start the first day in the front and who in the stern. Colton won. Every day from here on out at lunch, we would rotate positions, just as Sevareid and Port had. The crowd, which had grown to at least thirty people behind us, chuckled nervously as I let out an over-exaggerated groan to be starting the trip in the front. In truth, I grew to be quite indifferent as to which seat I was in. The front was relaxing and mindless while the back gave us something to focus on. Both, at times, desirable activities in a canoe.

The North Bay was loaded and already pushed halfway into the river. With one last look at the crowd and the cloud of steam rising from their cumulative breaths, I climbed into the front seat and grasped the cold wooden paddle with my numbed fingers. It felt like the paddle had a coat of slick ice around its handle. I heard Colton hop in behind me and felt, through my seat, the canoe push off from shore. We paddled several yards out of the small landing area and into the swollen brown river. Nearly at flood stage, the water was only a foot or two below the top of the riverbank, so very close to leaking over the edge onto the flat, forested, and sometimes swampy landscape that covers a majority of the Minnesota River valley.

"Take a right!" yelled Colton's father.

Out into the stiff current we paddled, inching forward at a snail's pace. The sight must have been depressing, almost laughable. Our friends and family standing on the riverbank watched helplessly as we, two skimpy eighteen-year-olds, paddled against the Minnesota River current, moving hardly two miles per hour. For over three hundred miles, we would continue this monotonous pace. They must have thought we had not a chance in the world.

"So… from here to Hudson Bay, huh?" I said to Colton.

He laughed. "Hudson Bay or bust."

For about five minutes, we paddled without a look back toward the landing, until finally, we gave in. The group had moved out to the riverbank and was still there, refusing to leave until our meager strokes pushed us out of sight.

Several of our closest friends drove down the busy highway running parallel to the river and hiked to the bank across from us at the first bend. They yelled pretty much what you would expect from any group of high school boys. Enough of the depressing goodbyes! After they threw some small rocks at us (playfully, of course), we turned the corner and they were out of sight. Suddenly, all was silent. We were alone.

"And here is where we hid our trolling motor," Colton joked.

It felt strange knowing what was ahead. We had taken a couple of long canoe trips before, and had spent countless hours in the past five weeks on the Minnesota River, so in a way, this felt no different. If I didn't know any better, I would have thought we were simply on another day trip. On the other hand, I was strangely nervous, as there was nothing in particular to be nervous about just yet. It just felt like it was impossible to *not* be nervous for something like this. The same thought that entered my mind when I walked to Colton's house earlier in the morning reappeared. We would see Hudson Bay before we would see home again.

It didn't take long for the cold to seep through our clothes and soak into our skin. All we had to keep us warm were our spring rain jackets, fleece sweatshirts, rain pants, winter hats, and paddling gloves that failed to even cover our entire fingers. Within fifteen minutes, neither of us could feel our hands. We knew all too well, however, that the only cure for cold was to keep moving.

Traditional paddling theory dictates that the bow and stern positions row on opposite sides of the craft, and the stern-man performs a smooth J-stroke at the close of each paddle stroke. The J-stroke is a subtle maneuver meant to negate the tendency for the canoe to turn in the opposite direction of the stern paddler's side, all by spinning the oar ninety degrees at the end of the rowing motion, and then holding it in the water for an extra second or two. Widely considered the most efficient method, we soon found that J-strokes would be impossible while traveling upstream. Even a one-second hold at the end of the maneuver brought us to a stop. Instead, the stern-man switched paddling sides as quickly as possible whenever a correction of course was warranted. We grew so accustomed to this method that it became standard practice for the length of the trip.

As we reached the small town of Carver, less than an hour into our paddle, we faced our first upriver rapids . . . and with an audience! The reporter from the *Chaska Herald*, who covered the most recent story of us, stood on top of an old railroad bridge that crossed the river directly above the rapids. In our practice runs, this little spot had given us a bit of trouble but was nevertheless quite do-able. The water this time was higher, though, and solely using brute strength, we would never be able to paddle up the center of this stretch. I'll admit, there were nervous thoughts that these rapids would be our extremely early demise. How embarrassing that would be to come home so quickly with a wrecked canoe.

As we approached, Colton expertly steered us through a back-eddy (a stretch of water just before a river bend near the inside-bank that actually flows in the opposite direction of the rest of the river in a sort of whirlpool) just to the left of the rapids. Our speed swiftly increased in the back-eddy as we barreled toward the bridge and fastwater, and just as quickly as all the pieces of this embarrassment-waiting-to-happen converged, we shot forcefully up into the side of the rapids, then quickly on through them to safety. Though the torrent below us pushed back, we, for the first time on the trip, leveraged Mother Nature to our benefit, passing her first quiz with perfect marks. Professionals could not have done it better! Being the overconfident lads that we were, our eyes remained forward without a backwards glance at the reporter. It was important we looked like we knew what we were doing.

As the day progressed, Colton began to complain of his stomach aching. In all honesty, I passed it off as nerves from first-day excitement. After all, my stomach tingled with nerves that I was sure felt no different.

Near 10:00 AM, we stopped for a break in a patch of weeds on the left side of the river. Within minutes, both of us were shivering uncontrollably despite the minor protection from wind the weeds created. Colton choked down half of his power bar before he and his stomach could handle it no more. He always did hate the power bars. Even I, one who typically enjoyed them, had to put forth an enormous effort to keep it down. I succeeded, knowing that I would later regret missing any opportunity to fill my appetite.

It wasn't until late morning that I finally appreciated the solitude that typically inspires me to venture into the outdoors. The morning rush had acted as adrenaline, adding excitement to the otherwise intentionally mundane activity of paddling a river. I began to notice the silence pressing my ears, along with the soft splash of oar into water and the bristle of prairie grass through wind like the hiss of a snake. Eventually, I noted the exceptional benefit of this moment being free of a cell phone or other technology. Too often a walk in the woods can be interrupted with a phone call or incessant need to respond to a text message. I was as much a perpetrator as any, but the prospect of "unplugging" for months was captivating.

In the town of Jordan, we stopped at a landing just below the County Road 11 Bridge for lunch. I shivered at the thought of our most recent experience at this bridge. Less than one month previous, on an embarrassingly unprepared practice run, we had concluded our day here in failure.

While our friends were working diligently in their last term of high school, Colton and I had itched to work the cobwebs off our Kevlar canoe. On one sunny morning with a temperature of roughly forty-five degrees (for Minnesotans, anything over forty degrees in the spring is shorts weather), we ignored the forecast that predicted an afternoon snowstorm and jumped at the opportunity to paddle the Minnesota River.

The practice run had been rather uneventful until just beyond the Carver Rapids, when all of a sudden, the blue skies transformed to grey. We were paddling so intensely that the swift temperature drop went unnoticed by us both. In no time at all, our light fleece outfits had gone from dry to completely soaked. What began with light rain had morphed into a heavy one. Then it began to freeze, turning to sleet, followed by a full-on blizzard. Colton and I experienced the full spectrum of Minnesota weather over the course of a mere thirty minutes. By the time we finally did reach the bridge in Jordan, our bones were drenched to the very core, and the wind had begun to gust through our wet fleece sweaters.

We pulled ashore and immediately retrieved a cellphone out of our waterproof pack. It's worth noting that on this practice run, we did not set up a ride back to our starting location at the park in Chaska, some nine miles downriver, wrongly anticipating that we would have been able to easily paddle back. Colton and I took turns calling our parents and friends to pick us up. To our dismay, all of our contacts were at school or work, and we were met with only their voicemails.

We were stranded. Our options were either to abandon our canoe and make the mile-long hike through the snowstorm into town, or to stay put and find cover to wait out the weather. In the end we found cover under the bridge, which any tornado-trained Midwesterner will tell you straight away is the worst possible option on a windy day, as bridges act as a funnel, effectively concentrating the wind into a smaller area. It didn't take long for the onset of hypothermia to hit.

Quickly noticing our minds beginning to blur and motor skills deteriorating, we scrapped our plan and hopped up to the topside of the bridge. Within ten steps towards town, our luck shifted; a vehicle approached and slowed as we frantically flagged it down. Through the snowflakes, we made out a man in the driver's seat rolling down his passenger window.

"You guys need a hand?" he called through the wind.

"Umm, think you can give us a ride into Jordan?" I asked almost pleadingly. Surely he could see the pain in our eyes.

Either sympathy or curiosity took over, and he allowed us into his truck. "It's really comin' down out there, eh? What are you boys doing out here?"

As we buckled up and closed the doors, Colton and I took turns explaining our upcoming trip to Hudson Bay, and that we were out on a practice run when the unexpected weather rolled in.

"Well, hopefully, you'll be better prepared on the actual trip, eh?" the man exclaimed, half chuckling and half scolding. He seemed genuinely excited about the Hudson Bay trip but equally worried. This was the typical sentiment from the majority of folks that we encountered.

Fast-forward one month, back at the Jordan Bridge, and we found ourselves again paddling through unfavorable conditions. This time, however, the snow from the morning had subsided, so we were at least dry. The temperature registered at twenty-nine degrees. The difference between today and our practice run was obvious: Jordan was not our destination but merely a lunch break nine miles into a 2,200-mile, multi-month adventure. To take our minds off the cold, we calculated that we were roughly in line with our planned pace for the day.

At the landing to the left of the bridge, there were two middle-aged men standing on the riverbank, pulling their motor boat onto its trailer.

"Looks like hard work," one said to us as we pulled ashore. I am not sure either of us responded. "Hard work" didn't quite do justice to our efforts. On the side of our canoe, by the bow, we had placed stickers reading "Minneapolis to Hudson Bay." Our friends at this landing must not have noticed, thinking we were simply high school kids playing hooky for a day on the water.

For lunch, we pulled out a bag of tortillas and made one peanut butter and tortilla sandwich each. It was a rotten meal, tasting exactly as you would imagine. This would be our first and only attempt at eating them. Our hopes were that perhaps a full stomach would help keep us warm. Hope, though, is a fickle friend, and after only fifteen minutes of sitting, attempting to swallow our sticky sandwiches, we were shivering once again and had no choice but to continue on our way.

The remainder of the day was miserable, with temperatures in the low thirties and limited talking. All that we spoke of was the fact that we were moving at a pace slightly faster than expected. Colton and I had been friends for twelve years, so silence wasn't new to our relationship.

By 4:00, while rounding a bend in the river, Colton spotted a bench on the left bank, and we decided it necessary for an early dinner break. Our hands were numb and stomachs empty from the minimal lunch. We pulled ashore and climbed the frozen mud bank. Unlike much of the Minnesota River, this specific location was in no danger of flooding over, with a remaining bank of nearly six feet in height even with the high water levels.

"What do you think? Noodles?" asked Colton, slumping down onto the bench. Sore from sitting on the wicker canoe seat all day, I paced around the bench and took in our surroundings. It was clear that we were still in the earliest of spring, as the lack of leaves and underbrush made the forest seem deceptively sparse.

"Sure, noodles are fine," I finally said and began digging through our food pack. One pound of plain spaghetti noodles – boring but filling. It was the standard dinner on our previous summer's trip along the Minnesota-Canadian border, so we stuck with it. For a few minutes we stood around, staring at the miniature pot atop our camp stove, waiting for the water to boil. Once our hands began to shake, impatience got the best of us and we threw the whole box of noodles into the lukewarm water.

Colton's stomachache was growing worse, so he lay down on the ground behind the bench, curled into a ball beneath his raincoat, and fell asleep. Standing still did little to improve the stinging cold that gripped my body, so I decided to take a walk. As it turned out, we were cooking at a campsite made for a scenic hiking trail following the east bank of the river. At the moment, the trail was not so scenic. Upon my return to the bench after only a cursory walk, I sat down on the ground with my back to a tree and shivered.

"Hey, Sean, I think the noodles are as done as they're gonna be."

I opened my eyes. Unintentionally, I had fallen asleep on the ground, leaving the noodles to cook themselves.

"How long have I been out?" I asked, wiping my eyes.

"No idea," said Colton, his own eyes red with bags beneath them. "I was asleep too. But the noodles have been cooking for a while and I'm starving. What about you?"

I nodded and stood up, using the thick tree behind me for support. "Are they ready?"

Colton stuck a fork into the pot, snatched a noodle, and gave it a taste. "Eh, the middle's still pretty hard. What do you think?"

"Screw it," I said. "I gotta eat." We dug in. Our stomachs had gotten the best of us.

Four bites was all it took. I turned away and faced the river on the verge of puking, but only gagged. At the exact same moment, however, I heard the horrible sound of a soft solid splashing upon the frozen ground behind me. I turned around to find Colton keeling over, throwing up his day's rations.

We sat in silence for several moments afterward, unsure of what to say. So many thoughts were rushing through my head. Without a doubt, the glamour from our morning departure was long gone. We were alone now. I realized that Colton's complaints of an upset stomach might have been true after all. Granted, the half-cooked noodles hardly helped the case, but his flushed cheeks and drooping eyes told me there was something more.

Finally, I broke the quiet. "Well, think we should finish early today and camp here?" On our previous trips, we would usually count on getting two or three more hours of paddling in after dinner. I could not realistically see us replicating that practice today.

Colton nodded dejectedly. "I'll go set up the tent."

I cleaned up the cooking gear and dumped the noodles before helping Colton with the tent. We had practiced setting it up at home, but somehow now the tangled mess of rods and snaps eluded us. Within only days, we would be able to set up in under thirty seconds, but tonight we cursed the engineers who designed the thing. Finally erecting it, we were both in the tent by 6:00 PM, bundled up in our sleeping bags.

It would be the first of many hungry nights, each one its own lesson in the class of outdoor survival. In an attempt to save space and weight, we chose to leave sleeping pads behind and regretted it already. The tent floor, waterproof as it was, provided little separation from the frozen ground and our sleeping bags, lowering our body temperatures at night drastically.

Colton kept the zipper open all night, sleeping with his head and shoulders stuck out into the tent's entrance vestibule, puking and dry heaving to no end. We each lay there, unable to sleep, secretly with the same thought. *What were we getting ourselves into?*

CHAPTER 3

Skunks, Stomach Flu, and a Sunken Canoe

Our reality, thirteen hours after falling into a warm slumber on night one, was anything but cozy. On the alarm clock that had been gifted to us years prior, the temperature read twenty-five degrees. We knew that summer would arrive eventually, and we were confident that our rationale for leaving so early in the year had initially made sense. Sevareid and Port left in mid-June and arrived at York Factory in late September as winter dangerously approached. In all, it took the pair ninety-eight days to finish, not including the added week it took just to paddle up a nearby river to the nearest civilization: train tracks heading south. Unsure of our exact pace or escape route from Hudson Bay yet (as far as we knew, we would be paddling up the same nearby river to Gillam, a town close to Sevareid and Port's exit which wasn't created until the 1960s), we estimated our completion to be somewhere around seventy days. Leaving a bit of room for error, we hoped to finish in late July or early August, arriving in the Arctic tundra during summer's warmest months. The cold was miserable now, but it could be deadly if it reached us in the far north.

While allowing Colton his time to awake, I made my way to our cooking gear, which was resting peacefully atop the bench where we left it the night before. The remains from dinner lay frozen to the dirt at the bench's feet. Out of curiosity, I scrambled down the steep bank to where our canoe was beached ashore. Just behind the stern seat, I noticed a puddle of water two to three inches deep on the canoe floor. No, I was mistaken. This might have been a puddle when we had gone to sleep, but what remained now was a block of ice, frozen through to the bottom.

An hour later on the water, life was not much warmer. Although the sun peeked through the tops of the barren trees, our hands were numb of feeling as we held the frost-covered paddles. The current was no easier to fight than the day previous, and we were beginning to run off of fumes. I thought back to my last several meals: a half-bowl of cereal at home that I was too nervous to finish before leaving to Colton's house, a few bites of a tortilla and peanut butter sandwich that I was too cold to finish, and four forkfuls of plain noodles that I was too sick to finish. Colton's meals mirrored mine but on an even lighter scale. This morning, unable to muster the energy to cook breakfast, we had each choked down a few handfuls of dry Cheerios, washed down by ice-cold water.

At one particularly strong point of current, a small dirt road passed by high atop the right-side bank with a small viewing deck. Standing at the deck was a man beside his red pick-up truck, to whom we originally paid little notice.

"You the two boys from Chaska canoeing up to Hudson Bay?" he called down to us through the silent morning air.

With our focus entirely on paddling hard enough to continue moving forward in the strong current, we half-heartedly responded in unison with a "Yep!" He bade us good luck and we mumbled our thanks, likely seeming rude. We were not used to people recognizing us and had not yet learned the proper etiquette or skill that goes along with showing gratitude for support while continuing to focus our energy to the task at hand. This skill would come with time and practice. Minutes later, I wondered how this man knew of us, and eventually decided that he must be a subscriber to the *Chaska Herald*.

By the time we reached the Highway 25 Bridge just outside of Belle Plaine, a town of around seven thousand residents, Colton's energy level was nil. Technically speaking, he was making paddling strokes, which were in essence his canoe paddle dipping into the water and out in one fluid motion. It was evident that it was not with the same vigor as it had been for the first several hours of day one. When you paddle with the same person for hundreds of miles over the course of several years, you begin to grow accustomed to their paddling ability. Colton was one of the strongest canoeists I knew, which generally (unless you are taking part in a true "race"), results almost exclusively from hard work. This was not Colton's best paddling.

"I need to stop," he groaned as we approached the bridge. There was a large and luxurious-looking landing on the right bank.

"Yeah… that's fine," I said calmly from the stern and steered us ashore. We both knew that there was no point in wasting my energy to make limited progress and risk burning out before Colton was back to full strength.

"I think I just need to eat," Colton said as he hopped out of his seat, pulling the canoe and me up onto shore with him, a routine of second nature for any experienced paddling duo.

"Rice it is!" I said.

While unpacking, a man with a camera jogged down and introduced himself as a reporter with the local newspaper. He snapped a picture or two of us posing by our canoe and asked me several questions before being on his way. Evidently, this man was also a reader of the *Chaska Herald*, as he seemed to know a good deal already about the trip.

I took the liberty of starting up a cup of rice for the two of us while Colton disappeared to curl up on a grassy knoll beneath the shade of an oak tree. While cooking, a second man drove down to the landing. In contrast to the reporter, the new visitor, it seemed, was not aware of our story. He made his way to our grass mound to see what we were up to just as the rice was finishing. Once again, I did most of the talking, and for good reason. Several bites into the rice, Colton vomited, sitting only an arm's length away from the complete stranger. Instead of sympathy, the man looked down at Colton as though he were a bug needing to be stepped on, and didn't say a word. Trying to laugh off the situation, I sarcastically asked Colton how he was feeling.

"Been better," he mumbled while leaning on all fours. In one motion, he backed away from his mess, turned around onto his back, and rested his hands upon his chest with eyes closed. It appeared we would be here for some time. The stranger, who never quite seemed interested in us to begin with, apparently grew bored and departed with a semi-cheerful goodbye.

"Well, what now?" I asked, doing my best to come across sympathetic, which I truly was.

"Dunno," muttered Colton, eyes still closed. "Honestly, I don't have the energy to go much further right now. And until I can keep down a meal, I don't see that changing."

I nodded. Upset as I was, I could not in good conscience blame Colton for his illness. Of course it was not his fault; he was sick! But hardly more than twenty-four hours into our trip, I was itching to continue forward. Without speaking, we came to an agreement: our health and rest came first, *and then* we would continue on our way. To keep going despite our health would jeopardize the entire expedition.

While Colton napped and attempted to regain himself, I devoured my portion of the rice and then washed off our dishes at the water's edge. We couldn't actually use the river water, as the Minnesota River in 2008 was considered to be one of the top five most polluted rivers in the United States. Collecting water from 17,000 square miles of southern Minnesota, which primarily consists of commercial farmland, evidence of runoff from animal waste, fertilizer, and pesticides was abundant. Later on, it was not uncommon to see drainage pipes leading right into the river, or to witness cows and other farm animals relieve themselves along the shore. I often worried that even touching the water would result in a skin-eating rash. For this reason, instead of filtering from the river for drinking and cooking, we consumed water from our five-gallon jug, filled in towns as needed.

At the riverbank, I heard the sound of a car engine making its way down the landing road. It was Colton's father, wondering why we were beached already, and on such a beautiful day! He had taken up an offer from a local pilot to fly over the river and snap some pictures of us. While in the air, Dan noticed that we weren't on the water, as expected, but resting upon shore during the mid-morning hours of only our second day. The weather had improved throughout the morning and now was in stark contrast to the day previous, sunny and near sixty degrees. Just our luck that the day we couldn't travel held the perfect weather for paddling.

Colton filled in his father while I sat in the grass next to him, pulling out individual blades from the ground and inspecting them closely. It was something of a family moment, so I didn't want to seem like I was intruding, though the fate of the conversation bore heavy impact on the future of our trip.

"Well, what're you gonna do?" asked Dan after Colton concluded his story with the most recent vomiting incident.

Colton sat in silence, eventually shrugging, disheartened.

I spoke up. "We'll just have to wait it out here until he's ready to move on. What else can we do?" Going home was not an option, despite it being less than a thirty-minute drive. Dan understood; he knew there was no way we were giving up just yet.

Likely in an attempt to lighten the mood, or simply to raise our level of motivation, Dan reached through his open car window and pulled out a rolled up newspaper – the *Star Tribune*. Nick Coleman's article about us had already been published and was the feature story on the front page of the Metro Section! I understood how the onlooker earlier this day had recognized us: our story was statewide.

"Can't quit now," Colton murmured after he and I both read the article. His voice held a sense of both relief and agony.

"Nope," I said. "Sure can't."

After Dan left, we sat separately; me in the sun by the river and Colton in the shade by the trees. The day was truly shaping up to be a beauty as I lounged on shore wearing only a pair of gym shorts. At one point during the afternoon, a man named Bruce visited the river with his young son and was absolutely thrilled to meet Colton and me. He had lost his lower limbs in an automobile accident earlier in life and spoke of his everlasting love for the outdoors. While the young boy played with their puppy by the water, Bruce re-lived his past adventures with me, including paddling trips on the Yukon River in Alaska. I listened wide-eyed; his level of commitment and determination through all odds was astounding. Stranger yet, though, was that Bruce's level of interest with Colton and me equaled mine with him. He had read our article in the *Star Tribune* and right away knew that he wanted to meet us. It was our first feeling of "fame," and it was strange beyond belief.

After bidding farewell to Bruce and his son, Colton and I took a hike several hundred feet into the woods, still clear of underbrush, to pitch our tent. It was very early and we had accomplished less than four miles of paddling during the day, yet we remained exhausted. A good night's sleep couldn't hurt us, as we knew that would be a rare commodity in the near future. I went to sleep with the hope that Colton would be feeling better tomorrow, and if not, very soon.

Our third day can be best told through my journal entry:
Day 3,

Colton was feeling better today. We got up, had a quick pancake breakfast, and got on the river by 8:30 AM. Current was strong but it was warm out, so not miserable. Muscles are starting to get sore. Got lost in a swamp trying to cut through a section of the river where it doubles back close to itself. Had lunch there. While near small town of Blakely during a particularly fast stretch of current, a chopper for KARE 11 News flew over us in circles for about five minutes taking shots of us paddling. Had to stop and rest for several minutes on one fast stretch because we were going backwards against the current and strong wind. Put back in and cut off almost 2 miles by portaging across only a few hundred yards of land. Saw a skunk there. Made it to Henderson and we are camping near a river-dike in town.

Drop the paddle in, pull back, and lift up. Drop it in, pull back, and lift up. Switch hands, drop the paddle in, pull back, and lift up.

Life on the river is mostly uneventful. A deer here, a rabbit there, and a gust of wind to be cursed by both of us took up a majority of the time. Days on the water were spent thinking, staring at the shore slowly creeping by, watching tiny particles in the water glisten in the sun before the paddle sliced into the brown murky depths below. It was depressing to watch the water move so quickly past, and the shore move so slow. Paddling upstream was like running up a downward-moving escalator. If we didn't paddle our hardest every second, we would go backwards.

Every couple of hours, we would find overhanging branches to cling to, providing a short five-minute break to examine the map and drink from our Nalgene bottles. There was no real reason for checking our location, other than to interrupt the monotony and to emotionally confirm progress. If we knew where we were, then we could calculate how fast we were traveling, and more importantly, how far we would get in that day. Apparently, boredom makes arithmetic fun for even the most mediocre of math students. We used enough algebraic equations that it seemed only fair we should have received some type of grade bump on our high school transcripts. After all, school was technically still in session.

As our schedule on the river became more refined, so did our routines. Being the light sleeper of the two, I had the pleasure of waking up the instant the alarm would sound at sun-up, and I swear sometimes even a couple of seconds before. It was then my job to wake up Colton, go outside into the cold air, hop around a bit with my hands warming in my pants, and then come back inside the tent to push Colton awake for a second and sometimes third time. As a continuation from previous trips, an unspoken agreement assigned Colton as cook and me as dishwasher. I despised washing dishes, but Colton seemed to revel in his cooking skills, so I was a good sport. Eventually, I grew to enjoy the handful of minutes spent crouched like a baseball catcher in front of our portable stove, watching Colton cook as though my famished stare increased productivity.

Breakfast was usually rushed. A few small pancakes each coated with peanut butter would suffice, and then swiftly onto the water. At first, and especially in the cold, the heat from our stove was so extreme that the crust of the pancakes would burn before the doughy core had a chance to cook. Within short order, though, Colton mastered a method of lifting and lowering the pan above the flame that would have made the Teppanyaki chefs at any local hibachi restaurant envious.

By lunchtime, the cold morning air would transform into a blistering spring heat wave, and we were ready to revisit the shore to feel the comfort of shade. Indeed, the forty-degree swings we experienced between twilight and high noon had recalibrated our internal thermometers. On the lunch menu was a cup of rice and six crackers each, which filled our stomachs only to the point of momentary satisfaction. Before long, the hour-long lunch breaks became our moments to live for. To sit and listen to nature at its finest, untouched by civilization, was nirvana.

At sundown, when it became too dark to see, we would pull ashore, set up the tent, and eat a tortilla stuffed with pre-cooked chicken, which came packaged in vacuum-sealed bags, much like tuna packets. Our mothers had found them at the local grocery stores before we left, and snuck a few into our food pack despite our insistence that plain noodles would suffice. After the first night's debacle, noodles were permanently barred from the menu, and we made an emergency plea home for new shipments of the chicken packets. Later on, in the Montevideo and Winnipeg layovers, our parents would deliver the entire stock of pre-cooked chicken from each of Chaska's major grocery stores. Every night, dinner was spent either in our sleeping bags with the florescent glow of a hand-cranked flashlight or atop the shore of the meandering river, so long as the dropping sun obliged our requests for extra light. Then it was off to bed, only to wake up and do it all over again. Like I said, routines became life.

For months leading up to the trip, we had planned out our first week's meals, estimated each day's progress, and envisioned the miles passing by smoothly. What we forgot was that things never go as expected, especially when such scrupulous plans are made. We should have known that wilderness travel is never as predictable as it seems from the friendly confines of home. By the end of the third day, our backs ached from sitting upright on wicker seats for twelve hours, and the muscles in our arms screamed at us to lay off the upriver paddling and provide time for them to recoup. The sun began to do its work on our upper bodies, as although the nights were cool, the days scorched ultraviolet rays onto our exposed torsos, the river providing nothing in the way of shade. Sunscreen only helped so much.

Skunks, Stomach Flu, and a Sunken Canoe

Colton's nagging illness persisted on and off into day four, proving to be an unexpected foe. Halfway between the town of Le Sueur and St. Peter, his health took a turn for the worse. Either a stomach bug or food poisoning was doing a number to his immune system, and his energy levels had reached an all-time low. I could tell he was miserable. Each hour we continued on, Colton grew more and more unsure of his ability to complete the trip. He didn't verbalize his concerns, but I knew. Conversation with one another was essentially non-existent, and what words he did say told me quite frankly that he didn't know how long he could last in these conditions. I did my best to remain optimistic and hoped that the positive vibes would give him the confidence he needed to continue. It was all I could do.

At a point where the river ran within less than a hundred feet from Minnesota State Highway 169, we gave in. Stashing our canoe and more cumbersome belongings, we hiked out to the highway carrying a survival bag with our wallets, phones, and tent. Thumbs out, we searched for a ride into town.

After waiting in vain for nearly an hour along the riverside highway, we finally hitched a ride from a young woman driving to Iowa. Generously, she dropped us off seven miles upstream in the town of St. Peter, an old river community that had been wiped clean from a disastrous tornado that swept through the area in the spring of 1998. Dozens of injuries, the tragic death of a young boy, and hundreds of thousands of dollars in repair costs burdened the town afterward. Ten years later, when Colton and I strolled through, you would hardly know that anything of the sort had taken place. Beautifully reconstructed, St. Peter sits on the western shores of the Minnesota River and rises gracefully up its bluffs, where there lies a small private college. We had been through the town before but knew little of what it had to offer; specifically, how it could be of any help to Colton, who desperately needed it.

In the year 1857, only four years after the creation of St. Peter, an attempt was made to change the Territory of Minnesota's capital from St. Paul to this more centrally located settlement. At the time, the governor of the territory, Willis Gorman, owned the land that St. Peter sat atop and looked to prosper greatly off of the potential move. After both of Minnesota's legislative houses passed the bill to move the capital, legend has it that then chair of the Territorial Council's Enrolled Bills Committee, Joseph Rolette, seized the bill and holed up in a hotel drinking whiskey until the legislative session ended, pocket vetoing the bill before Governor Gorman ever had a chance to sign it.

Knowing diddlysquat about how close St. Peter really was to being Minnesota's capital, we put our minds instead to finding a hospital or doctor's office that could give Colton the care he needed. As luck would have it, during our aimless wander down Main Street in long johns and sweats, an elderly man took pity on us and asked if we needed help. While driving us the several miles to the hospital in town, he informed us that he had missed his AA meeting that was supposed to have taken place that morning at the church downtown, and wished to make up for it by doing his "good deed of the day." His good deed may have saved our trip.

"When's the last time you boys showered?" asked the young receptionist, sitting safely behind her desk in the St. Peter Urgent Care lobby, clearly attempting to keep her distance.

"Been almost a week," said Colton in almost a satisfied sort of voice.

The receptionist seemed to have noticed his tone. "Trying to break a record?"

Before Colton had the chance to give his retort, I stepped in. "Ma'am, you may not be able to tell from the look of him, but my friend here is sick. Has been for a few days now. We're not sure with what, but he keeps throwing up. Can't keep any food down and has no energy. We're on a trip, though, where it's kinda necessary to, you know, eat and have energy."

"I'll have you sign in here and you can follow me when you're ready," she said, smiling politely. Under her breath, I could have sworn I heard something along the lines of her being sick too if she had to live with that stink.

Minutes turned into an hour, which turned into three hours of waiting in the small lobby while Colton moved from room to room, likely being tested for every possible disease known to mankind. I had read each magazine available, even the home decorating ones that nobody seems to read. The smell of clean, sterilized rubber that accompanies every hospital had soaked into my nostrils to the point where I could no longer smell the body odor of my five-day-old attire. A clock on the wall seemed to laugh tauntingly as time moved by at a painfully slow pace.

Every possible scenario played through my mind. Could Colton continue? If so, how long until he could? If not, what would I do? Should I keep on alone, making only a couple miles of progress per day until school was out for everybody, and then have a different friend join me? It wasn't until I had thought about *who* else would join me that I realized just how selfish I was being. Colton was sick, and all that I could think about was how I was going to continue on. It hadn't once crossed my mind if Colton was okay, simply for his own well-being. Just as I made up my mind to no longer think about my options and the trip until I knew that he was okay, a female doctor, not much older than the receptionist, opened the door that Colton had disappeared through hours earlier.

"You can come see him now," she said somberly. Something about her voice worried me. When I walked into a small room at the end of the hall, I was shocked at what I saw.

"What do you think?" exclaimed Colton, lifting his arms gently from the hospital bed to show off a spider web of tubes connected to him. He looked downright proud. "They've got me all hooked up. Apparently, I was pretty dehydrated, so they're just pumpin' some fluids in right now. Doc said I'll be good to go in no time!"

"You're okay?" I asked tentatively. I wasn't sure what kind of drugs they might have poured into his system. His mood was so lifted that I thought for a moment he might just jump off of the bed and do the Macarena.

"'Course I am. Gave Courtney a near fit."

"I bet," I said, sitting down on the doctor's "spinny-chair" next to the bed. It squished down ever so slightly beneath my slender frame. I let out a collective sigh that seemed to release the pent-up worries of the previous week. All would be okay.

The doctors at St. Peter's Urgent Care took pity on us, buying Colton and me a night's stay at a local motel. We decided it would be smart to give Colton's body an extra full day's rest before setting off again, so we chipped in and paid for a second night. A few of our friends made the short car ride and gave us company, lifting Colton's spirits further. Finally, nearly two full days after leaving the canoe, our friends drove us back to our outfit of gear and vessel lying just downstream of town and watched us paddle away, back up the current.

The town of Mankato, fifteen miles south of St. Peter, is steeped with a tumultuous history surrounding the Native Dakota tribe. After a treaty was forged and signed between the US government and the local Dakota in the mid-1800's, which traded over one million acres of land to the United States in exchange for food and money, officials in the region charged with handling the exchange instead sold the food to white settlers and pocketed the cash. With many Dakota starving and desperate, a small group of them attacked the settlers in 1862, killing five and stealing their eggs. Later that night, bands of Dakota attacked entire white settlements, killing upwards of eight hundred locals in what is now known as the Sioux Uprising. The Dakota War of 1862 followed for several months throughout the region, until finally the United States military stepped in.

Upon the surrender of the Dakota, thousands of their combatants were captured and tried for their participation in the fighting. Initially, over three hundred were sentenced to death, but after Abraham Lincoln stepped in and pardoned all but the most severe perpetrators, thirty-eight were left to be hanged in downtown Mankato. It remains today as the largest government-sanctioned execution in United States history. Instead of disregarding this facet of the town's history, Mankato has faced the incident head-on, naming the plot of land at the hanging's location "Reconciliation Park."

In Mankato, we faced what we would eventually crown as a "Top Three Toughest Up-Current Stretch" of the whole trip. Paddling through downtown, the river switched directions geographically, and instead of traveling southwest as we had for the first six days, we began our northwestern climb towards the South Dakota border. Not only was this a significant geographic point of the river, but just upstream from the city, the Blue Earth River flowed in, nearly doubling the strength of the current downstream of the confluence.

Underneath the first of two bridges through downtown, we took a break to collect ourselves and discuss the best plan of attack. After a rigorous brainstorming session, we decided to follow the right shore, where hopefully, the current would be the slowest. We made it twenty feet.

"Okay, that was Plan A. What's Plan B?" I asked, frantically wedging my paddle between two rocks on shore in a valiant but fruitless effort to prevent us from losing ground.

Colton cursed under his breath. He and I both knew the answer: lining. Imagine pulling a one-hundred-fifty-pound person up a rocky incline with rope, while the dragged person did everything in their power to prevent you from moving forward. Now imagine that person is your canoe, and you might begin to understand lining upstream. Fortunately, we had two of us pulling the canoe; unfortunately, our one-hundred-fifty-pound outfit was quite the fighter.

The progress we made lining was faster than we did paddling, but just barely. Due to simple physics, the nose of the canoe was constantly pulled closer in to shore, where it would get caught up in the tangled shrubs that extended several feet into the river. For this reason, only one of us could pull the canoe, while the other was left with the job of pushing the nose of our boat out with a paddle away from obstructions.

Not only was lining slow moving, but boy, was it painful. On both sides of the river, cutting through downtown Mankato, the banks were filled in with large rocks, creating a man-made levee of necessarily loose footing. While the rocks worked superbly for keeping the levee sturdy, they were also a broken ankle waiting to happen for anybody foolish enough to walk on them. Between the rocks were agonizingly sharp shrubs that punished any aforementioned fools who were dense enough to walk through with bare legs. Let it be known that we were indeed dense fools. Within only minutes of walking through the levee, our legs were covered in bloody scratches.

Over an hour after the start of this formidable stretch, the current subsided only slightly, and so we once again changed plans and decided to try our odds with the river. It was better. Not good, but better. Eventually, we reached the confluence with the Blue Earth River, and the difference was noticed almost immediately. Only several feet after we passed the intersection, the current slowed considerably. In an instant, our morale made another leap. The sun was shining, fighting the current was no longer a seemingly impossible battle, and Colton's stomach was finally feeling better. Perhaps we weren't in so far over our heads after all.

We never spoke of it, but both of us knew that passing the Blue Earth River in Mankato was a turning point. Only two days prior, holed up in St. Peter, our trip seemed to be destined for failure. Now I could tell Colton's optimism had shifted entirely. During one of our many silences, Colton broke it with words that confirmed my thoughts. "You know what?" he said. "Believe it or not, I'm having the time of my life."

A mere trickle compared to its prehistoric counterpart, River Warren, the Minnesota River meanders its way through a valley carved ten thousand years ago, which at times reaches five miles wide and two hundred and fifty feet deep. Through much of the land between the Twin Cities and Mankato, the river valley is so great that enormous farms and major cities lie between its bluffs. Between Mankato and the river's source at Big Stone Lake, however, the valley grows smaller, and consists of forest, sparse farms, and rolling grassy hills that would fit nicely in a Scottish countryside.

Near the tiny town of Judson, only noticeable to us due to its bridge, we decided to make camp. Colton's parents and his girlfriend were supposed to meet us with our finished food-box and a few supplies.

Pulling ashore, Colton hopped out of the bow first and began pulling the canoe up the bank. It was the same, simple routine that we had mastered throughout all of our trips. As the bow was pulled upward and over the height of the bank, the stern reacted conversely, thrust beneath the water with me aboard. Within a matter of seconds, the entire back end of our North Bay was submerged beneath the river surface, along with my legs, waist, and our tent pack. I instinctively scampered up the canoe, over the packs, and dove onto shore in a move that would surely be presented in slow motion if recreated in a Hollywood action movie.

Together, we pulled the now half-sunken canoe out of the river and took account of our belongings. Something was missing. To our panic, we noticed the dry-pack carrying our tent floating peacefully away, down the river.

"Sean! Grab a stick! Or a paddle!" Colton yelled. We were frantic. It would be an embarrassing conversation with our parents to describe the reason for needing a new tent as "it floated away." No, if anything, we would risk swimming in the pesticide-infested river to save it. With Colton holding on to a semi-sturdy tree with one arm and the back of my shirt with his other, I reached out over the water with a paddle and gradually coaxed the dry pack to shore.

Once all was settled and saved, we took a moment to consider what had just happened and began laughing hysterically. Here we were on a grand adventure, "The explorers from the Cities," and we could hardly pull the canoe ashore without screwing something up. What was better was that surely cars passing on the nearby bridge, or the two groups of folks landing their boats with ease across the river, had seen our struggle. If the story was leaked to reporters (we convinced ourselves that we were noteworthy enough for this to be plausible, which of course, we weren't), our version, we decided, would include heroic acts including but not limited to: baby saving, world saving, and girlfriend saving.

After pitching the tent and setting out our wet luggage to dry, we trekked through the woods to a gravel road. Not long after, Colton's mother, father, and girlfriend showed up. We rode to a nearby restaurant and feasted on a "real meal." It was great to see family, even if they were technically not mine, and it was obvious that it was an additional boost for Colton. Along with the newly finished aluminum food-box, we were given more chicken packets, power bars, and even a new waterproof camera donated to us by one of Colton's mother's coworkers.

When the Wittes left, and we hiked back through the woods to our tent, we noticed an odd detachment from the rest of the world. It was as if we were on our own all along, and the short bouts with civilization were small dreams – a distraction from our real lives in the wild.

CHAPTER 4

Wilderness Could Wait

Minnesota spring is an erratic and unpredictable force. The days are hot and sunny, the nights bring a wintry chill, and the difference between the two causes a volatile storm season. Interestingly, we were well prepared for rain and dangerous storms, mentally if nothing else. It was the sun and cold that was our true enemy. We would have complained more to reporters about the sunburn and frostbite, but the sunburn was our fault for often neglecting sunscreen, and the frostbite made us sound tough.

As we neared the city of New Ulm, yet another bit of evidence proved spring was upon us. On several occasions, the river flooded over the banks and extended through the trees as far as the eye could see. Since the majority of our days were spent on the river, this was rarely an issue. Only when it was time to cook at noon or camp at night did this pose a problem, forcing us to postpone, on several occasions, our much-longed-for breaks.

An advantage of the rising water, however, did surface. Floods provided an occasional solution to paddling up the agonizingly winding river. When the river doubled back on itself, creating a severe oxbow, we sometimes had the opportunity to simply leave the river and paddle over land, effectively eliminating up to a mile of our upstream battle. While passing through New Ulm, there was one point that we cut off over two miles of up-river torture through a flooded connection no longer than twenty feet. It was truly glorious.

Typical of traveling through towns, Colton and I were the subject of many "gawkers," as we began calling them. It was a beautiful day, and the river was home to an abundance of recreation, most notably fishing. Many of these anglers, casting from shore, looked at us as we paddled up the current as though we were not two young men, but animals from a zoo, out for a day's leisurely paddle.

At the far end of town, nearing dusk, we stopped at a landing filled with a rambunctious group of teenage boys. Skeptical as we were with this crowded location, the conditions of the flooding river meant we couldn't pass up the opportunity for high ground to camp. To our surprise, a woman whom we had previously labeled a "gawker" several miles earlier was at the landing, apparently waiting for us with an older gentleman. The two of them approached us, introducing themselves as Virginia (Ginny) and Jim. As it turns out, they had been in contact with our parents through email and were waiting for us to pass through. Ginny had, in fact, experienced her share of outdoor adventure several years prior, paddling down the entire Mississippi River… twice!

Jim and Ginny invited us into town to the small club where they worked, called Turner Hall (which evidently was something of a bar/restaurant/men's club/gymnastics studio/banquet hall). We, of course, accepted. While there, Ginny and Jim treated Colton and me as their own, buying us dinner while a local reporter came by for an interview. By now, we were already growing accustomed to reporters and interviews, but the experiences that we had while participating in them remained fascinating nonetheless. Many of the reporters that we met with seemed truly intrigued and, at times, downright envious of us. There were others, though, that clearly did not believe in us, did not find our trip newsworthy, or had no idea where Hudson Bay was. The reporter from New Ulm seemed to be a representation for at least one of the latter characteristics. He much preferred to speak about hockey, basketball, and the history of New Ulm, which was actually a pleasant change! Regardless of the level of interest reporters showed in us, much of our publicity could be attributed to these local papers, and for that, we grew quite grateful.

Recent word from Colton's mother was that donations were starting to pour in through a website she created, where followers could track our progress through the SPOT Messenger updates and news stories. The donations, we hoped, would eventually be enough to buy us a floatplane ride out of York Factory, saving a week of grunt work back upstream to Gillam.

The remainder of our night was spent mingling with guests at the bar. They all seemed amazed by our trip, and picked our brains with questions throughout the evening. Many had heard of us through the news or word of mouth, and several had been following along intently. It was odd to have people be so honored to meet us, all because of an adventure that, quite honestly, was for our own indulgence. We were of course honored beyond belief that people were taking such notice in us, but remained confused as to why anybody would care about a canoe trip that two teenage city boys were taking. It seemed that so many talked of trips they had dreamt of completing, but never did, and we eventually concluded that most were simply jealous!

At ten o'clock, we called it a night and set up a tent in the park next door to Turner Hall. For once, we were sleeping on soft, flat ground, free of roots and rocks. The only concern now was lying on our aching, sunburnt torsos.

A recurring phenomenon for us both was a certain delirium at night caused perhaps by hours of silence and solitude. Dreams began to grow indistinguishable from reality. For as long as I could remember, Colton had been an avid sleep-talker and, on occasion, sleepwalker. During the countless sleepovers that we had growing up, I would be hard pressed to find a night that Colton did not talk in his sleep. There were even times, according to our parents, that we had talked to each other in our sleep. Up to this point, however, perhaps because we were sleeping so heavily from the day's activities, neither of us had heard a rumble of sleep-conversation. In the late hours of this night, however, I was awakened by a sharp and heavy pain on my sunburnt stomach. Colton was sitting up, facing me with his arm outstretched. He had just karate chopped me awake.

"Sean! The water – the field is flooding!" Colton was yelling frantically, looking out of our small tent windows. Having just woken up, I jumped up to look outside. Within a matter of seconds, I realized the absurdity of this possibility. We were at least one hundred feet above the river, camped up on top of the bluffs. If the field were underwater, so then would be the entire town of New Ulm.

"Colton, there's no water. It's not even raining." I said back, slightly annoyed, but more-so amused by the look on his face. Looking around sheepishly, he thought about a retort for a moment, and then went back to sleep without another word.

Leaving New Ulm, the weather was fantastic and the river felt tame. That lasted ten whole minutes. Seemingly out of nowhere, a navy blue wall of cloud appeared to the southwest. The feeling of impending doom crept in as we watched the storm crawl nearer; there was an almost peaceful feeling to it. I remember thinking, more as a mental note, that I would never forget the sight. One doesn't truly respect Mother Nature until being entirely within her mercy.

Before we knew it, the thunderhead was upon us, a torrential downpour smashing the already swollen river. We hastily threw on our raingear and continued along. Of course, paddling through rain was not a problem and is to be expected from time to time with expedition canoeing. One cannot be so blessed as to be handed dry weather every day. Unfortunately, though, it was not long before lightning began to flash and thunder rolled in. This was the last straw; through snow, hail, wind, rain, or cold we would paddle, but to be on the water during a lightning storm bordered on lunacy.

The Minnesota River was not going to let us go without a fight. With the water spilling over the riverbanks and stretching to the bluffs, it took almost an hour of fearful paddling through the storm before we found high ground near a bridge. We pulled the canoe through a small patch of weeds to shore and hiked to the road. For thirty minutes, we sat in the ditch just above the riverbank and watched cars drive by, huddled together in our raingear. When we eyed the direction that the storm came in from, there appeared to be no end in sight.

Finally, a grey minivan drove by and the occupants rolled down their windows, asking if we wanted a ride to any place dry. At first, we thanked them deeply but declined the offer, as the day was still young and the storms would hopefully pass.

"The radio is saying that the storms will be around all day," said the driver, a middle-aged male. We looked at each other for a moment. The offer of escape was awfully tempting.

"Okay, do you know where Turner Hall is?" we asked.

The driver looked around to see if anybody in the vehicle knew... all blank faces. "Nope, but if it's in New Ulm, we'd be happy to bring you there. You'll just have to show us the way." The kindness of strangers was truly amazing.

As guilty as we felt for taking our third layover day in less than two weeks, it would have been useless, not to mention miserable, to hunker down on the side of the street all day in the rain. Promptly, we hid our canoe as best we could in the weeds and harnessed it to a few trees in case the water rose while we were away. The rest of our gear we packed into the family's minivan and squeezed our wet selves into the farthest back seats. In the front seats were the driver and his wife, with their twenty-something daughter in the middle row, and what we assumed was her daughter, a young baby, next to her.

After some casual conversation, we found that this family was traveling from the Twin Cities to the father's parents' home in New Ulm. Upon hearing about our trip, they were very interested and asked many of the same questions. "Where do you sleep?" "What do you eat?" "How much weight have you lost?" And the most common of them all, which as luck would have it, was the only one we did not have a good answer for yet: "Why?"

At the entrance to Turner Hall, a man whom we met the night before, Ron, stood in the doorway, laughing through thick coughing bouts. "Back already?!" he called.

"Yeah," we said back, embarrassed but slightly appreciative as to the humor of the situation. "Mind if we hang out here today if the weather stays bad? This family asked if we needed a ride anywhere and this is the only place that we know of in town."

"Not a problem, not a problem," said Ron, still laughing. "Just toss your stuff in the back where it's out of the way."

We thanked the family for the lift and carried our gear inside. Back in the bar, we turned on the weather channel and saw there were indeed storms in the forecast for the remainder of the day. The workers at Turner Hall continued to treat us like family; Jim came back over with dry shirts, and Ginny provided us with free food and drink. Ron, though we never actually found out what he did there, sat at the bar and gave us good company. After another delicious meal, we offered to re-pay Ginny for her kindness by filing some paperwork. Their bills weren't run through a computer system, so our menial task was to sort them by category. It was easy but time-consuming, which was perfect. We were used to spending our days working non-stop, and to do anything less felt unproductive.

Until around four o'clock in the afternoon, Turner Hall sat empty, so we had ample time to relax in the sauna and use up excess energy in their workout facility. Later, we went upstairs into a ballroom next to the gymnastics studio to throw around our Frisbee. In the studio, a lesson full of girls kept looking oddly at us, as if it wasn't normal for two eighteen-year-old, scruffy-looking boys to play Frisbee in the ballroom.

As the dinner and bar crowd rolled in, we continued our mingling from the night before. There were some whom we had already met, but most of the people were new, and their conversations just as interesting. Throughout the night, we got to know two of the bartenders, Mario and Lucy. We also met two sisters who had family on Big Stone Lake in Ortonville, where we would be paddling through in a week or two's time. Near the end of the night, there was a group of ten elderly German men who came in. They were from New Ulm but had recently been traveling around Minnesota singing folk songs as something of a hobby. Of the two songs they sang us, one was oddly dedicated solely to Colton. As he blushed a special shade of red, I laughed with mirth on the stool next to him.

We decided that it was foolish to pass through these towns, with so much culture and so many interesting people, without embracing them. This was an adventure, and while the key intent of our trip was to escape from civilization, we realized that in Minnesota, in the year 2008, escape was not possible. So, we made a compromise. The first half of our trip, up until the city of Winnipeg, would be devoted to discovering the two-legged creatures along the river, to learn their stories, and to hopefully make many new friends. Discovering the wild could be saved for the second half, after Winnipeg, where wilderness would be inescapable.

In the weeks leading up to our late-April departure, both Colton and I received a great deal of advice suggesting we find some type of "cause" to dedicate toward our expedition. In the midst of our relentless search for sponsors that could help us with the mounting trip expenses, we were very close to taking heed.

"What kind of cause did you have in mind?" I asked one outdoor expedition expert, after hearing this suggestion for the umpteenth time.

"Well, the Minnesota River was recently named to the list of top five most polluted rivers in the United States, and I'm guessing the Red River isn't much better. Maybe you could document the pollution levels, and use this as a platform to spread environmental awareness."

Environmental awareness... this was always the option. Colton and I were both staunch environmentalists. How could we not be, considering the gift Mother Nature has provided us? But there was something in a cause that didn't fit with our objective for the trip. We wanted, simply enough, to find adventure in a time when many believed it no longer existed. While environmental advocacy would have surely benefited our finances, it added a complex element to a trip whose crux was something simple: a boyhood dream.

In the end, we declined all suggestions to add a "cause." Sure, we were in the same act declining all possible sponsorships, but that mattered little to us. We hoped instead that our stories of the river's pollution would suffice in raising awareness of the environmental degradation taking place.

Just beyond New Ulm, we began to more frequently witness the Minnesota River pollution first hand, regardless of our lack of cause. During lunch one day between New Ulm and Redwood Falls, we stopped at a small boat launch that seemed to be privately owned, as it stood directly next to a field of soybean crops. While eating our chicken tortillas, we marveled at how the crops of this field, just like several others we had passed in recent days, grew up to the river without a natural buffer, providing free rein for pesticide runoff. Far from farming or environment experts, something about this still struck us as careless. To the farmer's defense, spring flooding had caused water levels to rise dramatically, so we were hopeful this was not a normal occurrence.

Later in the same day, Colton's red cap that he claimed to use for sun protection, but which I knew full well to be another bizarre fashion statement in classic Colton style, was blown into the river. After spending the previous two weeks fighting for every inch of progress against the current as though our lives depended on it, Colton now begged and pleaded to turn back and retrieve the thing. Clearly there was some type of sentimental value to the hat, so I swallowed my pride and turned our boat around.

It was the first time in as many weeks that we paddled with the current. Our canoe felt like a racecar. Each paddle stroke pushed us at least twenty feet! Within seconds, we were back to Colton's hat, which was floating peacefully down the mucky river.

"How fun was that – going downstream?" Colton exclaimed. While I agreed wholeheartedly, it was obvious he was attempting to distract me from the impending paddle back up river.

"You better really love that hat," I said, smiling through gritted teeth. Just over one week in, and small annoyances began to creep up on us about the other. Friends and paddling partners for so long, we each expected this to occur, so it was easy, for now, to set the irritations aside.

On a large rock ledge one afternoon, two men lounging by the river met us enthusiastically. We soon came to realize that we were speaking with the Mayor of Redwood Falls and a photographer for the local newspaper. The mayor greeted us with keys to his city, something that frankly I didn't know existed in real life. He also spoke candidly about how excited he was to finally meet us in person, and that although we would likely forget this encounter in no time, he would remember it for the rest of his life. Naturally, we disagreed.

"So tell me about those crickets then!" the mayor bellowed unexpectedly.

We looked at each other, bewildered. Up until now, we had a pretty good grasp on what was said about us in the news, and the crickets had never been mentioned. How then, did these men know about our childish senior prank?

"I've been saying since I first read about you two boys, I've been saying I wanted to meet you..." the mayor talked with such excitement. "But then, the other day, I read the new article in the *Star Tribune* about that prank you guys pulled on your last day of school. Ha! I knew then that I *had* to meet you!"

"What article? We haven't been interviewed by them since our first day. How would they have known?" Colton asked.

"They interviewed your mother," said the mayor, nodding towards Colton.

"Oh boy." Colton's head sank.

It felt peculiar to have people we had never met, including all readers and subscribers of the largest newspaper in Minnesota, know more about us than we were aware.

After bidding the mayor and photographer farewell, the afternoon grew excessively warm, and our outfits dwindled to only our gym shorts. If the water hadn't been so polluted, and ice cold, we would have been tempted to jump in.

Just as we began to seriously consider breaking for a cool dip, a car drove by on a road running parallel to the river that until then, we didn't know existed. It came from upriver, and before we knew it, the noise vanished behind us. Within the course of one minute, we found ourselves back in society with the rumbling of machine engines, only to re-enter the serenity of nature again after the noise died out. We were reminded of just how close our adventure was to civilization.

Fifty feet ahead, the river turned left and there was a discrete gravel landing on the right shore. As we approached the landing, we jumped out of our silent stupor from the sound of a loud crunch against the bottom of our canoe.

"Crap," said Colton. "A sandbar."

In 1930, when Sevareid and Port traversed the same river, North America was suffering from one of the most severe droughts of all time. Because of the drought, the Minnesota River was flowing at a record low, and sandbars had been a constant struggle. For Colton and me, in the midst of spring floods, they were about the last thing we worried about, just ahead of aliens and asteroids.

Nevertheless, we were stuck. Stabbing our paddles into the ground, we tried desperately to push our vessel loose from the immovable bottom. For several minutes, we attempted to push forward, so steadfast in our goal of moving upstream.

Out of nowhere, the same car that had awoken us from our wilderness slumber minutes earlier arrived at the landing, only feet away. Out the door scrambled four teenage girls, about our age, shrieking with excitement.

"Are you the boys from the Cities?" they yelled. It appeared that they were entirely unaware of our sandbar predicament.

"Yep, that's us," we called back, continuing our struggle to break free.

"We've been reading all of the articles about you!" the driver of the car said. All four of them had their cell phones in hand.

"Could we get a picture of you?" said another, holding up her phone, ready for a picture on the spot. "We were hoping we'd see you paddle by!"

I looked at Colton in disbelief. This had to be the handiwork of our friends from back home, playing a prank. No way did we have *groupies*.

"Uhh… sure," I said, suddenly trying to stay as cool as possible, like this was standard for us.

"Could you pose?" the driver asked. Each girl had walked down to the riverbank.

Coming to a re-realization that we were still stuck, and shirtless, we kept our paddles pushed into the sandbar but cleverly rested our arms on top of the oars and gave hearty smiles. This must be how supermodels felt.

The girls left quickly after the pictures were snapped, and we finally figured out that the obvious way to set ourselves free of the sandbar would be to push backwards with the current. Never had we felt so famous and so foolish in one moment.

Wilderness Could Wait

The first planned layover day for Montevideo was timed to coincide with Mother's Day – about two weeks into our journey. After fourteen days, we were supposed to have traveled far enough to reach the last town on the Minnesota River. Due to a lingering illness, a hospital visit, and storms, we were behind. In a crunch, we hoped instead to land in Granite Falls, a town just fifteen miles downriver from Montevideo, in time for our parents' arrival. A downpour of rain soaked our coats and pants, and dripped down our still premature stubble as we neared Granite Falls. It is remarkable how rain can so literally dampen the spirits of a wilderness traveler. Knowing that this day would be our last before the layover, our minds drifted easily to thoughts of a warm bed and full bellies.

For lunch, we pulled off into a riverside park, still several miles from our destination. There was a small pile of firewood soaking in the rain next to the landing, and upon further examination, we noticed a smeared sign with our names and a phone number to call. It turned out one of the rangers for the park offered up the firewood for us to take, which we graciously declined. The thought was heartwarming, but the wood was drenched and would take days of hauling around, keeping it out of the rain, to dry out.

Granite Falls was home to a series of obstacles, and we imagined that this was the furthest point upriver steamboats could have traveled during the latter half of the 19th century. In reality, steamboat travel on the Minnesota River was only prevalent for two decades, and even then, Mankato was about as far as the boats felt it necessary to travel. By the time there was a worthwhile destination west of New Ulm, trains were the transportation of choice in southern Minnesota, marking the quick demise of steamboats on the already shallow river.

Two miles downriver of Granite Falls, while portaging around one such obstacle known as Minnesota Falls, I watched through the rain ahead of me as Colton carried the canoe upside down over his shoulders. During our practice trip the summer before, I vowed to never portage a canoe again. Even our Bell North Bay, weighing in at only forty-five pounds, was a miserable experience. Instead, on portages that we chose to sweep in one run, I always volunteered to carry both of our packs, one on my back and the other on my front, with two straps on each shoulder. Sure, my load was heavier, but I detested the constant act of balancing the canoe over my head and the limited vision with the bow restricting my field of view. Colton was happy with the compromise, and so was I.

Walking along the blacktop shoulder that ended abruptly before falling into the grassy ditch below, Colton seemed to be rather enjoying his temporary relief from rain beneath the canoe. Just as I was about to call for a break to catch my own rain-free moment, I watched as the canoe made a sharp jerk downwards, followed by a loud howl from Colton. He threw the canoe off his head and let it tumble down the ditch to our right.

I looked at him incredulously. For a second, it appeared he had tripped and then overreacted by taking his anger out on our fragile boat. After grabbing the top of his head, followed by a curse under his breath, I realized that perhaps this was more than a simple stumble.

"The thwart just snapped over my shoulders," said Colton, keeling over a puddle on the rugged pavement.

I looked down the ditch to our canoe, lying peacefully at the bottom, face up. The floor was gradually collecting rain beneath the knee-high grass. In the middle of the canoe, stretching from gunnel to gunnel, the wooden beam that held two shoulder pads was snapped at its midpoint. Somehow, the added stress of the miscellaneous gear we had strapped to the seats during the portage was too much for the thwart to handle.

For a minute, we wallowed in our misfortune. The North Bay had been our canoe for nearly a decade, and neither the thwart nor the gunnel had so much as cracked. Now, in the rain along a mile-long portage, it chose to break clean in two. Eventually, we came to the realization that we were lucky for this to have happened now, five miles from Granite Falls, instead of in Northern Manitoba, hundreds of miles from a hint of civilization.

Our only option going forward was to stash the canoe in the woods and hike along the road into town. Our parents could, once they met us in town, drive us back with the proper tools to fix it.

After thirty minutes of walking through what we were sure was an increasingly severe rainstorm, a man and his son pulled up beside us in a black pickup truck. We peered through the rain into the open window by the passenger seat.

"Colton? Sean? You boys look lost! The river is back that way," yelled the man inside, motioning behind him. He was Native American, with long black hair that came together seamlessly in the back as a properly fit ponytail.

We explained our situation.

"Hop in!" he exclaimed, pushing forward the passenger seat that was holding his teenage son, allowing us to climb into the backseat of his extended cab. As it turned out, our escort was the Tribal Chairman of the Upper Sioux Indian Community, the local tribe. He had read of our trip and could see the look of defeat gradually building in our eyes. It was beginning to feel as though the gods were against us with one setback after another on the Minnesota River. To make matters worse, Colton's wrist had been aching for days, and it was reaching the point of agony for him.

To convince us that the Spirits above were on our side, he gave us a gift of braided Sweet Grass. If things, most notably weather, seemed against us in the later days of our trip, we could burn the offering and pray to the gods of weather for better fortunes. We were so honored by his gesture that we never were able to get ourselves to burn the two-foot stock of grass, but instead made sure to keep it with us for the entirety of our journey.

Granite Falls, we found, was a beautiful riverside city built around the largest dam that we had yet encountered. Near the dam in the center of town, the lawns of gorgeous homes and quaint neighborhood streets lined the river shores. To the south, downriver of the dam, there sat the secluded Memorial Park, complete with a boat landing, an open-walled pavilion, fire pits, and a lengthy network of paved trails. It was in this park where we spent our layover day. Family, friends, and girlfriends joined us in lounging on the lawn, grilling hotdogs, and playing Frisbee. Our fathers took the liberty of fixing the now un-portage-able canoe. Arrogantly, we joked that they were our "pit-crew."

Locals who were following our story intermittently visited the river to say hello and pass on wishes of well-being. One woman even slipped us one hundred dollars but refused to give us her name. It was further evidence of the compassion of strangers.

By nightfall, our parents and friends were on the road back to Chaska, enjoying the end of their one-day vacation from the cozy lifestyle we had left behind weeks ago. Of course, sitting on a park bench within the pavilion, next to a roaring fire and beautiful river (the agony it put us through had temporarily slipped our minds), our current lifestyle was quite luxurious, if we did say so ourselves. Better yet, only feet behind us was our tent, set up on the flat concrete surface beneath a roof, baking in the heat from the flames nearby. It seemed impossible tonight to imagine any sort of misery on such an adventure.

We woke up a short while later on the frozen floor of the pavilion with a burnt out fire next to us. Once again, it was a cold morning. Breakfast was quick, as we knew that the only way for our hands, and ultimately our bodies, to warm up was to paddle. It was astonishing how quickly attitudes can change in the outdoors. Each night we would celebrate our triumphant victory over the day, thrilled to be on such a voyage. By the next morning, reality would hit hard that a new battle was upon us.

With our repaired canoe, we shoved off into the river, and for the second time of the trip, we pointed the bow downstream. Two days previous, when we attempted to hike around the falls, we expected to finish the portage and paddle into Granite Falls. Obviously, that plan didn't work out, and we were forced to hitch a ride into the city. There had already been and would be plenty more compromises on this trip when it came to warm meals or an occasional dry bed. We felt guilty enough about that, but if we were skipping river-sections, we figured there would be nothing left in our principles.

So down the river we paddled, only a couple of miles to the end of our failed portage. The canoe glided gracefully over the glass-like water, and the shore cruised past in a blur. Getting as close to the falls as we felt comfortable, we turned the canoe around and resumed the all-too-familiar battle against the current.

While passing Memorial Park again, our night's campsite, we

saw another group of fans waving us onward. Not long after, about a quarter mile before the dam, the current nearly doubled in speed. It was as though we were paddling up rapids again; progress was impossible. We looked at the dam ahead, which focused in our view by the straight river shore. The water spouted down menacingly, a clear attempt to prevent paddlers from nearing its dangerous bottom.

At first, we attempted to line the canoe up the left side of the river, but like in Mankato, thick shrubs made it painstaking to move along shore. We made our way then to the right shore for another lining attempt, and almost immediately, a submerged rock slipped out beneath my feet, dropping me waist deep into the icy water. My lower body went instantly numb, and all rational thought in my brain became frozen. For a moment, I stood bemused, oblivious to the dire situation at hand. Then, as quickly as I had fallen in, I found my arms pulling myself up onto shore, working quite independently of my conscious mind. I got out, looked at the rock that had succumbed to my paltry weight, and let out a shivering chuckle.

"That was close," I said, smiling sheepishly. Colton shook his head and laughed briefly. Fortunately, the sun was out and the day had begun to warm, so it wasn't long before I was dry to a comfortable level. We both knew, though, that clumsiness while lining could prove fatal in the north woods; the conditions there would be much less forgiving than these.

After some intense deliberation, we settled back with making another attempt along the left shoreline, and lost once again to the current; it was time to portage. Within a minute of unpacking, we found ourselves surrounded by news cameras, the mayor of Granite Falls, and several fans. As we walked, we spoke to the mayor and reporters, while the cameras shot us from various angles. It was getting to the point where moments like this now hardly registered as out of the norm. The cameras we were used to, and the mayor and fans were simply acquaintances from the day before with whom we were eager to continue conversation.

Once departing again on the up-current side of the dam, we noted our love of the towns that we passed through and the people we met, but there was something undeniably addicting about our life on the water. It was like a constant tug at our bodies and minds, pulling us back whenever we strayed.

CHAPTER 5

Epic Voyage

Beyond the approximately fifteen miles of river between Granite Falls and Montevideo, there would be less than a half-day paddle to our first lake, Lac Qui Parle. We intended to reach the lake the following day, so we set Montevideo as our goal for today. It was perhaps the windiest day of our trip yet, but for the first time that we could remember, the wind was predominantly at our backs. The stiff current was not totally overridden, but the help was gratefully accepted nonetheless.

At the first landing in Montevideo, we were greeted by another sign, posted with a phone number and short letter. It was from an environmental group called CURE (Clean Up our River Environment), and they were interested in meeting up. Upon calling the number, we made a deal that we would rendezvous at a bridge crossing, ten miles further upstream from Montevideo. After taking the previous day off, we weren't ready to call it a night quite yet, especially when we were making such good time at the behest of the wind.

A couple of miles after Montevideo, we came to a bend in the river where we noticed it would be possible to cut off a two-mile section littered with rapids, with a one-mile long but relatively simple portage. The last time we attempted this, Colton ended up with a bruise on his head and a broken canoe thwart. Confident that this go-around would be different, we pulled ashore and went ahead with the land-jump.

As daunting as a mile-long portage is to anybody that has attempted one, we welcomed it gladly as a chance to stretch our legs and give our arms some rest. Along the left side of the portage, there was a golf course with newly developed homes across the fairway. Once again, our adventurous spirits were forced to be put on hold, as the civilization we passed was a constant reminder that this was a far different region than it had been some seventy-eight years previous, when Sevareid and Port voyaged through this very area.

After the portage, the river became a skinny, winding mess, and it was difficult to gauge quite how fast we were going. Despite our unpredictable pace, within less than a minute of arriving at the remote bridge, the CURE folks drove up to meet us. There were three of them, all teachers, and they helped us stash some of our belongings in the woods before we hopped into their truck and headed into town.

Graciously, they treated us to a meal at a downtown pizza joint. This meal marked the beginning of two traditions that would persist for the remainder of our journey. First, after we ordered a second extra-large pizza (on our dollar, of course), we bagged it up to be eaten cold during the following days. We were so happy with adding a fourth menu option to our peanut-butter-pancakes, chicken wraps, and rice, that from here until the edge of the wilderness, every three or four days, we would pick up a pizza in whatever town seemed convenient. This practice later became the subject of a headline of a *Star Tribune* article while we were in Northern Manitoba.

In addition, two of the kind gentlemen that treated us to this meal were also avid outdoorsmen. One, named Butch, could not stop raving about our youthful exuberance. The other, who must have been in his mid to late twenties, was so excited with our trip that the only phrase he could muster that evening was "epic voyage." From this point on, that phrase became a cheer of triumph when we conquered the forces of nature or when we realized the absurdity of our adventure. Even if there was a point in which neither of us spoke for several hours, the icebreaker was typically for one to mutter, "Epic voyage," and then nothing more. I believe that those words got us through some of the more trying moments of the trip.

The next morning, Butch was kind enough to treat us to breakfast at a deli connected to the local grocery store. If one was to shape their view on the world simply from watching the evening news, they would conclude that human beings are awful creatures, out to get you around every corner. We were finding that it was the exact opposite. Many strangers went out of their way to lend a helping hand. I became certain that there was not a better way to learn about small-town America than a canoe journey through its core.

At breakfast, we read an article about us in a local paper based out of nearby Willmar. The author had interviewed us in Granite Falls during the layover, and the result was what Colton and I decided to be one of the best articles from the entire trip.

Butch watched with a smile as we read the piece. After we finished, he told us the most encouraging words we would hear. "You know, when I first heard about you guys, I thought, 'Oh just high school kids... they don't stand a chance. University of Minnesota championship swimmers and paddlers have attempted this trip and not made it much further than here.' Then Tom, the reporter that spoke with you guys in Granite Falls, he called me up after the interview and said, 'Butch, these guys are the real deal. They're something else.' And I believe he's right. If ever anybody could replicate Sevareid's trip, you guys are it." We swelled with pride.

Back at the river, Butch gave us a hearty farewell, and we were on our way. As though Mother Nature knew we were back on the water, she decided to punish us for our warm meals and stray into civilization. Within minutes, a downpour ensued and the temperature dropped to thirty-nine degrees. The rain soaked through our jackets to our freezing bodies, from which there was no escaping.

I remember wondering what the weather was like back home. It was a Tuesday, so our friends were in class, probably angry that they had to walk the hundred feet from their car to the school doors in the rain. It felt selfish, but I wondered if any of them were thinking about us. I doubted it, assuming our friends were instead enjoying their final weeks of high school before summer jobs and the real world. While a relaxing summer break with little responsibility seemed enticing, we truthfully would have chosen a summer paddling up a river instead.

As we passed a farmhouse on the left-hand shore, we noticed through the heavy rain a sign facing the water. Taking a lesson from experience, we understood this to be for us. There were few others traveling the river this time of year, and our location between towns was relatively remote. The sign held a "good luck" message and a list of names and numbers of people to call. Under a bridge a half mile further, we took refuge from the cold shower and, using my cell phone, with what little battery life was left and almost no reception, called the folks from the sign.

Under the bridge, a break from the rain was welcome, but the wind being funneled under it just as much counter-acted the respite from the rain, especially with our already soaked outfits. A man named Tom from Montevideo answered, saying that he had family in the area that could come out and meet us. We told him that it was not necessary, but we would be portaging over a bridge and dam within the hour and they could meet us there if they liked.

Sure enough, by the time we began our second trip around the dam that led into Lac Qui Parle Lake, a car rolled in and the occupants called us over. It was indeed Tom's parents, June and Todd, and they allowed our soaked selves to take shelter in their vehicle. As we spoke with them about our adventure, June treated us to delicious brownies. The ingredients were kept secret, though I am sure she would be a millionaire if ever released. Needless to say, it was a far cry from the fruit snacks and granola bars to which we had grown so accustomed.

After fifteen minutes of spoils, we grudgingly left the warm car and re-entered our wet reality. My fingers ached beneath the damp gloves, and I was glad they would at least avoid the cool wood of my paddle. Even so, the task would have been all the more daunting if it were back on that rotten river to fight more current. No, we had a lake to look forward to!

"What a sight for sore eyes!" said Colton as we loaded our canoe, squinting ahead to the vast water body before us. Even with the gusting wind that blew frigid rain and lake spray into our faces, our spirits grew high and hopeful.

On a river, when the wind blows, there typically isn't enough water surface for waves to accumulate. As we knew from previous trips, this was far from the case on lakes. We shouldn't have been surprised then, when the second we began lake paddling, our high spirits began sparring with three-foot breaking waves. An experienced canoeist can handle rolling swells without a problem, but when gusts blow heaps of the lake over the gunnels and into the canoe, even the best paddler in the world will face troubles.

The impression we received from several locals was that this lake was a marshy mess, so we were pleasantly surprised that Lac Qui Parle was instead so open and long that the far shore, our eventual destination, sat out of sight, beyond the curvature of the Earth. In the distance, a bridge could be made out across the horizon. Based off of our maps, we knew this to be more or less the halfway point of the lake.

By the end of our lunch break five miles up the shore, the rain had finally ceased, but the wind and cold remained. For sport, a new hobby that resembled one from Sevareid and Port's time on the Minnesota River was created. It was spawning season for carp, so the lake was littered with surfacing fish, perfectly camouflaged in the dark water and choppy waves. Once spotted, we swung our paddle downwards like poorly trained lumberjacks. It wasn't the sportiest way to fish, but we were hungry, the fish were carp, and we had bad aim. If I'm not mistaken, the most contact made all afternoon was my knuckle with the canoe's gunnel. A small scar was placed permanently on my left ring finger as a reward.

At long last we arrived, around 5:00 PM, at the lake-crossing bridge. The wind had not let up, and our bodies were drained. For a break, we beached our canoe at the gravel landing and hiked to a small building just off shore. We hoped that the building would have a television, or anything of the sort, that could indicate the remainder of the day's weather.

Upon entering, we immediately noticed the distinct smell of bait and found ourselves in a room the size of an average convenience store, except with a bar at the far end and long tables lining up and down through the middle of the floor.

A balding man wearing flannel came out from the back and introduced himself as Jason. "Anything I can help you with?" he asked.

"We're just paddling up the lake. Wondering if you guys have a TV that we could check to see how the weather is looking for the rest of today and tomorrow?" I asked as we wound our way through the tables to the bar.

Jason looked at us inquisitively, as though it wasn't a common occurrence to have two teenage boys in asking about the weather. "I can tell you now that the weather ain't shapin' up any time soon… at least not today. But if you like, you can check out for tomorrow." He snatched the TV remote off of the bar and turned the screen to the weather.

Making ourselves comfortable, we watched, waiting for the Weather Channel to move on to tomorrow. The wooden barstools we sat on rested unevenly on the floor, so that they tipped slightly with each shift of our weight. The rest of this day looked to be just as bad, if not worse. We anxiously rocked back and forth in the stools as we deliberated whether or not to press onward

"Where you headed?" Jason asked, breaking the several minutes' silence that had followed our debate.

"Um… Hudson Bay," we both said in unison, more as a question. It was always awkward to try and answer that one. Where were we headed? It made the trip seem so simple to give such a short answer. In a fitting response, just as we often expected, Jason opened his mouth slightly, closed it, and nodded his head. We clarified where Hudson Bay was, as that seemed to be the typical source of confusion, and left the conversation at that.

Upon seeing the remainder of the day's weather, we reluctantly decided to finish early. I felt lazy, but this time, our reason seemed legitimate, and we had worked our tails off all day. A break was well deserved.

Jason's mother, Jane, came out into the bar and chatted with us after we sat in silence a few more minutes. According to her, even if we wanted to continue on today, our chances of finishing the lake were slim to none, and from here on out camping was illegal due to some type of preserved wetland. Within an hour or two, the mother-son duo was gracious enough to feed us a delicious chicken dinner, free of charge.

As the night progressed, the bar filled in, serving as something of a hangout spot for local fishermen. While anglers came and went, we listened intently to some of their stories about the far northland. We stayed up into the wee hours of the night listening to two men rehash their journeys in the Canadian bush, hunting and fishing in the land where nature makes the rules. Our imaginations ran wild as we pictured ourselves in the north woods on similar adventures. It was impossible to believe that we would experience this on the same trip. Our adventures so far were fascinating but not unfamiliar. The land ahead was foreign, and there was no way for us to gauge just how dangerous, daunting, or exhilarating it would be.

We were lost. Or stuck. Either way, something had gone wrong.

"Is that the bridge we need to go under?"

"I don't know; it looks pretty low…"

"I think it is… look at the map."

"Well, how do we get there?"

"I don't know."

Marsh Lake: a sea of cattails that stretched as far as the eye could see. Entering the lake wasn't a problem. A hop, skip, and jump past Lac Qui Parle and we were there. Exiting the marsh, however, was proving to be slightly more difficult.

Our morning started off cold but calm, and blue skies on the forecast beckoned us onward. The stillness and lack of clouds on Marsh Lake was serene. We were surrounded completely by the sky and the water, so still that they had merged into one blue blanket. Ahead, all we could make out was a thin line of trees on the far shore.

As we neared the north shore, it became clear that we would have to first navigate our way through a maze of tall reeds that reminded me of the hedge mazes I attempted as a kid at local fairs. Upon our completion of the maze, we were disappointed to find that we had taken a wrong turn somewhere back, leading us to a dead end. At the fairs, I had been able to cheat by following the beaten path… not this time. Though our destination, a bridge marking the river's outlet, appeared to be no more than forty yards away, it was through a mess of mucky bog and snarled weeds.

"Think we can break through?" I said to Colton, thinking of my last resort on hedge mazes.

"Worth a try."

In an attempt to show supremacy over the marsh, we backed the canoe up, took aim, and charged. I'll give the weeds credit; they were stronger than they looked. We hit the wall of cattails with speed, giving us less than a canoe's length of progress before our momentum slowed, bringing our boat to an abrupt stop. The attempt at breaking through was laughable. Clearly, backtracking would be our only option.

Later on, out of the marsh and back onto the slick current of the narrow Minnesota, the river grew ever smaller and windier, until finally mirroring that of the unnavigable streams from back home. Eventually, based on advice from a park ranger back at Granite Falls, we portaged our boat over a dike into a large reservoir adjacent to the river. The portage was easy, and the current-less reservoir made for pleasant canoe travel initially. Our plan was to connect back up with the standard route on the far side of the man-made lake, effectively skipping one of the more tangled sections of the Minnesota River. Naturally, this plan would only work if we could find the connection back to the river, and after hours of circumnavigating the swamp border of the reservoir and finding no outlet, the pleasantries of flat-water paddling were replaced by panic.

"North is that way," I said, pointing to the opposite end of the lake.

"Yes, but the river is to the east."

I looked to where Colton was motioning and shook my head.

"That's south," I said. "East is that way."

Our debate grew heated for around sixty seconds before quickly subsiding with a bitter jab at the ranger who had sent us wayward. We found a common bond in deflecting blame for our own mishaps.

Indeed, our frustration had been simmering to a boil all day. The unrelenting sun combined with the confused tension of feeling lost twice in a day made me feel like I was going to snap at the next minor setback. Our only option to escape this mess was to backtrack to the dam that we entered the reservoir through. Following the reservoir's shore straight north from the dam, we made our way to the point where the lake was nearest the river, and once again pushed our craft into the dense border of marsh.

Thirty feet had never felt so far. In muck up to our chest, we waded through the sharp weeds. Having portaged over a dam to escape the river's wrath, it seemed ludicrous to fight so hard to return. Not only was the acrid smell of decomposing matter only inches from our nose and the footing impossible to navigate, but the thickness of the weeds made pulling the canoe through it all feel like we were attempting to squeeze a beach ball through a tightly woven knot-hole. Once finally connected to the river, we found a fallen tree lying just above the surface to help us climb back into the canoe.

The rest of the evening was spent navigating the river as it meandered through a ten-mile bog that filled the valley. Weeds stretched as far as the eye could see, with the only exception being a bit of hilly land in the distance to the right. The river wound like a snake through the flat bog.

Just before nightfall, we came upon a small gravel road that traveled right through the middle of the swamp. We couldn't tell if it was still under construction, or how often it was used, but after hiking it up and down for a few minutes, we deemed the road unwise to camp upon. The gravel could poke holes in our tent's waterproof floor, and if a car happened to come by in the middle of the night without seeing us, it would run us right over. This posed a problem, though; there was nowhere else to camp. Everything in sight, or at least within reach, was swampy and wet. After several minutes of researching the map, we found on the other side of the swamp what looked to be more high ground: a railroad track.

Back into the canoe we went. Thirty minutes and one hundred more feet of pulling through weeds later, we approached the tracks, desperate to set up camp as the sun dropped rapidly. We climbed the tracks to see if there was solid ground on the opposite side... negative. While there was a farm in sight, too much wetland sat between it and us to make it there tonight.

"What do you think, set up camp on the tracks?" Colton joked.

"It *is* the only flat spot."

I laughed. "Yeah, probably not the best..." A low rumbling in the distance suddenly cut me off.

The sound was unmistakable. We scampered off the railroad and into our canoe that had been beached just below the tracks, pushing the vessel off shore to sever our tie. It didn't take long for the rumbling to reach us. Soon, thousands of tons of steel on wheels rolled past, only feet away. The volume was beyond belief, and even though we weren't on shore, we could see the ground causing the water to ripple. For minutes, the train cruised by with a deafening roar.

"I'm gonna go with 'no' to the whole sleeping on the tracks idea," I said after the train finally passed.

A train track has a simple setup. There are the rails and timber ties themselves, which lie on top of baseball-sized rocks that stretch out five to ten feet on either side. At this particular spot in the tracks, immediately after the rocks, was a grassy slope down to the swamp. This slope was our home for the night.

"Well," I said, climbing awkwardly through the tent door, "hopefully one of those trains doesn't come through tonight. . ."

"SEAN! WAKE UP!"

A noise filled the tent so thickly that Colton, whose face was within inches of mine, couldn't yell loud enough for me to hear. It was as if a grenade had exploded just outside our tent, and the resulting boom was never-ending. Piercing red lights flashed by outside the tent walls, flickering through the otherwise dark night. A hurricane force wind blew on our tiny fabric home from the direction of the tracks, threatening to push us down the bank into the swamp. The look on Colton's face was pure horror, like he was staring death directly in the eye. His mouth moved, but no sounds came out, or at least they didn't reach my ears. He frantically made gestures to me with his arms in a motion that I assumed meant to hold the tent down.

"WHAT?!" I yelled back at the top of my lungs. It was fruitless; I was deaf to even my own voice.

Colton tried once again to yell, waving his arms hysterically, but it was no use. I had seen many expressions upon my best friend's face before, but this one was new. There was no frustration at my lack of understanding. No panic that he wore, like the night in New Ulm when he was convinced our tent was flooding. It was the look of a young man without hope, with nothing but the inevitability of death occupying his consciousness. He lay back down, at peace with his life and its fate, committed to his only chance at survival: to hold down the tent.

I looked outside our small window. Still, all that could be made out were the flashing red lights that blinked by like a strobe light in a haunted house. A piercing sound of metal on metal saturated the night air. Groggy and so startled from the abrupt awakening, it took until this moment to finally realize what was happening. A train was passing us, only feet away, at cruising speed. Assuming that Colton's orders were to hold the tent down, I moved to the corner where the wind blew incessantly and sat, staring out of the window.

Never have I been more uncomfortable. It wasn't the discomfort of a long car ride, but more that of a soldier walking through no-man's-land, waiting helplessly for a shell to rain down upon them at any instant. Obviously, we were far from the danger of a soldier, but the feeling of vulnerability must have been similar. It seemed that at any moment, the train could derail, bringing our lives to a crushing end. This, I assumed, was Colton's worry as well. There had only been a handful of train derailments throughout all of the United States in the early 21st century, but having just woken up, my mind was not thinking rationally. I wanted nothing more than to be home, in a safe bed, as far away from this place as could be.

"Shaken," is the clearest description of our emotions the morning after the train fiasco. Breakfast was spent sitting on the tracks, regrouping and discussing the night's events. The fear in Colton's eyes became clear to me: he had been dreaming about the previous night's joke when the train woke us, and that we had actually camped out on the tracks. Apparently, the soundless yelling was his warning to lie parallel to the rails, our only shot at surviving the impossible circumstance.

We sat in silence for a bit after breakfast, listening to the constant buzz of crickets chirping in the cool morning air. Foggy clouds of our breath was the only motion in sight. Colton recorded a short video on our digital camera as evidence of the night's camp. Our demeanor epitomized much of the trip: cold, hungry, and quiet, all the while with an air of lightheartedness through forced attempts at humor.

Our last day on the Minnesota River was spent navigating the tiny creek, its flow shrinking further than the day prior. Due to the low frequency of traffic on this section of the river, we were forced to maneuver around logjams every hundred feet. At first, these minor obstacles were simple, little more than a thirty-second delay as we pulled our outfit effortlessly over the jam. As the morning progressed, however, we were faced more and more commonly with entire trees blocking our way. Further along yet, the logjams ceased, but the river became shallow and littered with sandbars.

"Almost there," I repeated to myself. Only hours more and this river would be nothing more than a distant memory. Ortonville, just a couple of miles further upstream, meant the end of the Minnesota River, and the end of fighting the current. We were close enough to reach out and grab it.

As we neared Ortonville and the lake, oddly, we came to a four-way intersection in the river, our minds drawing quite a blank. Seldom do river travelers find themselves at a crossroads, yet here we were. Stretching perpendicular to our stream was a large, man-made canal, flowing downstream from right to left. Straight ahead, across the canal, was a continuation of the stream we had been struggling against all morning. The canal to the right was long and straight, with an obvious current that would be a bear to fight. Given the width, though, it appeared too large for it not to be cleared of logjams. After some deliberation with our map (which failed to show this intersection), a compass, and several "what's-the-worst-that-could-happen?" scenarios, we decided to follow the canal upstream.

Whether the canal was the best choice or not was never actually decided. While it would eventually bring us to the proper destination, a strong current did exist, and it was pushing us back down the river fiercely. We eventually beat it, however, and gradually, the prairie backdrop beyond the tall riverbanks transformed into the outskirts of a town. It felt like we had gone back in time a full century; the buildings and homes were of a style more suitable to the late 1800s.

At the far end of the rustic village, the river traveled beneath an old dirt road bridge, cutting under it through a stone archway. Beyond the bridge and straight ahead, we could see the dam that marked the entrance into Big Stone Lake. Under the archway, the river was condensed to less than ten feet wide, naturally creating a Venturi effect, a strong force of water funneled through a small gap. The current was unbelievable, beyond anything we had faced yet. With the end in sight, it was almost poetic.

It took us nearly five minutes of vicious paddling to pass beneath the road. Perhaps it was possible to turn back and portage over the bridge, but this was the last fight of a river growing increasingly desperate to defeat us. We would not give in.

Once past the tunnel, the remaining distance to the dam came easily and with cheers of triumph. We were at the source of the Minnesota River.

Blue skies and a slight breeze called us onward. Big Stone Lake runs twenty-two miles along the Minnesota-South Dakota border. To the west, in South Dakota, rolling hills and sparse trees dominated the landscape, while wooded cabins filled the Minnesota shore. The lake itself remained about one mile wide for its entirety. Lying at the south end of the lake, the small town of Ortonville and its few restaurants called to us longingly, but Browns Valley and the continental divide at the north end was too near to rest. From Browns Valley on north, the water flows up the continent towards the Arctic. Lake Traverse is Big Stone Lake's squatter, less refined, little sibling. Out of Lake Traverse, water flows into Mud Lake, which in turn deposits itself into the Bois de Sioux River. North flowing for only forty miles, the Bois de Sioux becomes the Red River of the North when the Otter Tail River joins its ranks. Beyond the Red River lies Lake Winnipeg, and after that the ensuing bush country rivers of northern Canada, all the way to Hudson Bay. The tug to continue was like gravity, and who were we to oppose a law set forth by Isaac Newton?

After an abbreviated interview with a local reporter, we pushed off of the rocky beach in Ortonville, gliding peacefully onto the blue water of Big Stone Lake. Perhaps it was our imagination, but compared to the cloudy brown of the Minnesota River, its waters were downright pristine.

Wind rolled onto the lake from the open hills of the western shore, bringing with it slow-rolling waves that were, for the first time that I could remember, welcome. They did little to slow our progress, and with the sun shining and our spirits bright, we laughed in joy as our canoe bobbed up and down like a cork in the waves.

Early on in our annual trips to the Boundary Waters, Colton and I learned the proper way to navigate wavy waters. It didn't come easy, and many close calls taught us quickly the absolute wrong ways to do it. Common canoeing knowledge dictates that paddling directly against waves, or at a minimum, quartering them at a forty-five-degree angle are the safest ways to go about traveling on a windy day, but when the wind is coming perpendicular to your direction of travel, going out of the way to quarter with and against the wind can be a time-consuming burden. We countered that, as long as it's done properly, paddling at a ninety-degree broadside angle to the waves is not only faster, but safer.

Many lake paddling accidents occur when canoeists are forced to broadside waves, and they either tip or take on water as a result of incorrect weight shifting. It's natural when a swell meets you from the side to want to lean towards it, worried that it will tip you and your canoe over in the direction the wave is heading. But that instinct attempts to break the laws of physics, an almost always futile proposition. Each canoe is built to maintain a level surface on the water, including when waves push it to an angle. Thus, when the rolling wave reaches the canoe, the proper course of action is to instead maintain loose and free hips, and let the boat do the work, trusting it will bob over the wave as it was designed to do. By the time we reached Big Stone Lake, using the "loose-hips" method was second nature.

Near suppertime, we had neared the north side of the lake, and the shoreline lost the already limited trees it had on both sides. Knee high grass grew across the ridge that stretched hundreds of feet above the water. By the end, the bluffs rose ahead on all three shores, giving us the impression of paddling along the bottom of a large stadium. In my head, I imagined the natural amphitheater filled with cheering fans, applauding our conquest of the Minnesota River basin. They egged us onward, exclaiming that the hardest part was over, and it was all downhill from here. A celebration song echoed over the fans, like the music that plays after a home run at a Major League Baseball game.

Reality came back to me abruptly and the grassy bluffs were empty, but for a small white shack halfway up the Minnesota side. There is no real glory for wilderness adventurers. In towns, we were minor celebrities, meeting reporters, cooking lunch next to camera crews, signing autographs, and shaking hands. It was always very exciting, and the continued support was humbling. But back in the wild, there would be no crowds, no fans. When it would be needed the most, we knew all we would have was each other. Together, Colton and I had paddled up the basin of Glacial River Warren, but while it was all "downhill" from here, the true trials of the wild remained ahead.

CHAPTER 6

The Shifts

The sun rose gently over the east bank of the Bois de Sioux River. Our view from the opposite shore was immaculate, and the peace it accompanied was divine. It would be an hour at least before the sun's heat could blanket the flat landscape of the Minnesota and North Dakota border. Less than a mile to the west, across a sea of dirt, was the town of Fairmount, North Dakota. Near a bridge leading to town, a lone billboard stood beside the road advertising land for sale at one dollar per acre to help spur development. Leading up to this point, the vast fields were a farmer's "God's Country."

Forty miles of straightened and manufactured stream, the Bois de Sioux is the southernmost source of the Hudson Bay Watershed. To Colton and me, all this meant was downstream paddling. Of course, "downstream" may be a bit of an exaggeration. The Bois de Sioux, and eventually the Red River of the North, which is the predominant border river of Minnesota and North Dakota, travels across the flattest region in the United States. With an average drop of one to three inches per mile, we were essentially traveling the length of a long, skinny lake. The drop in elevation on the Red River was so minimal that we heard a number of locals compare the slope to placing a piece of paper under one end of an eight-foot-long two-by-four.

To make matters worse, the tree population along the Bois de Sioux River was sparse at best, so wind howled through our drainage ditch with little remorse. Perhaps months from now, the fields on both sides would be filled with corn stalks, adding at least another six feet of wind protection. In May, however, we were not so fortunate.

The day prior began at Lake Traverse, our unofficial start of the downstream descent to the Bay. Like Sevareid and Port, we had the fortune of meeting good Samaritans with a truck in Browns Valley, providing us help in the portage over the continental divide. We could have turned down the help, but that would have been rude, and our backs ached something special. That night, we slept at a small but beautifully crafted hunting resort in Browns Valley. In the morning, after listening to our hosts' warnings of mosquitos and mud, we were off.

Our jaunt across Lake Traverse and then Mud Lake was uneventful, save a morning phone interview with a Twin Cities radio show. Our cell reception was terrible and the wind, coupled with using the speakerphone, caused what I'm sure was terrible entertainment for those listening. Most of the five-minute interview consisted of hardly audible questions, followed by Colton and me responding with "what?" and then a chorus of laughter on the other end. We'll never be sure, but we had the distinct feeling that their amusement was at our expense. Not giving it another thought, we shut off the technology and basked in the beauty of our battery-free adventure ahead.

After the dam at the north end of Mud Lake, the Bois de Sioux officially began. Historically, this tiny stream was a natural border between Minnesota and South Dakota for five miles, after which it became the Minnesota and North Dakota border instead. While the original streambed remains the official border, the Army Corps of Engineers straightened the river into the ditch it is today as a by-product of the construction of the Reservation Dam and the White Rock Dam, at the north ends of Lake Traverse and Mud Lake respectively. Collectively called the Lake Traverse Project, this transformation was made for recreational and flood control purposes in the 1940s. Colton and I, however, were more concerned with the straight river ahead, which appeared to have as few curves as it had trees on its shores. The wind blew through the tiny basin at our faces, building up force like a gust beneath a bridge. By 6:00 PM, near Fairmount, we had enough and called it a day.

The Shifts

The next day, while watching the sun rise at our camp near Fairmount, I remembered that at the same time our friends back home would be completing an annual charity event in which they walk the track at school and camp out on the football field, in order to raise money pledged for cancer research. The event had a distinct energy to it each year, the result of an honorable cause paired with the fact that it was mid-May, only weeks from summer vacation. A year earlier, we were with them, playing touch football and listening to Colton play guitar by the tents. Everyone stayed up to watch the sun rise above the eastern horizon. Looking out over the open plains, it was comforting and strange to know that they were watching the same sunrise as Colton and I.

This morning marked the start of a much-anticipated portion of our voyage. We called it "The Shifts." For various reasons, high school girlfriends and an itch to reach the north woods being two of them, we decided to paddle one at a time nonstop, in twelve-hour segments, for the duration of the Bois de Sioux and Red River. One would paddle from 1:00 AM to 1:00 PM, and the other from 1:00 PM to 1:00 AM, while the non-paddler would lie in the front of the canoe to eat, sleep, and rest.

In theory, the shifts made sense. No longer fighting the current, one person could now paddle farther in twenty-four hours than two could in twelve. In Colton's mind, at least, the debate was as simple as that. As an added bonus, I was also looking forward to the twelve hours of rest per day, far more than we had been getting prior.

"Whoever starts today will have a short shift, and then will get the one that starts at 1:00 AM tonight..." said Colton, trailing off. "Kind of an even trade-off, right?"

I laughed. The 1:00 AM shift was the proverbial graveyard shift. "Sure," I said. "That's even, as long as you get to be the one that does it."

Per our pre-trip protocol for disagreements or major decisions, we tossed the nearest flip-able object, in this case, a book. I chose front cover side up, and Colton chose its back. I lost. For some time, I maintained that the front cover had more weight, so it wasn't a fair toss. Regardless, I wore the honorable badge of inaugural shift paddler to start the day.

The wind from the previous day had subsided, allowing us a pleasant morning as we stroked north towards the confluence of the Bois de Sioux and Otter Tail rivers. Where they meet, in the towns of Wahpeton and Breckenridge (the former on the North Dakota side, the latter in Minnesota), the Red River of the North would officially begin. As the crow flies, we were about fifteen miles to the confluence and were confident that this could be easily achieved by lunch. This would not be so. After slumping behind our estimation, we quickly adapted our mileage estimations by about double to account for what was a far windier riverbed after Fairmount, as compared to the man-made portion to its south. We wound up generalizing that fifteen crow miles equated to thirty miles on the river, a fact that frustrated us to no end.

Aside from the winding course, Colton and I spent the morning delighted by the beautiful weather. After passing a couple of landmarks to confirm our pace, we basked in the glory of confirmation that we had correctly guessed how the shifts would yield more miles-per-day than paddling together for shorter stints.

Colton, now lying lavishly in the bow, was so thrilled with his newfound free time that his inner-monologue became uncontrollably outward. Randomly, he would point out with enthusiasm every idea that popped into his head.

"At this rate, we could finish the trip before school is out back home!" he exclaimed. "What if Hudson Bay is still frozen by the time we get there?"

"I should really be using this time to tan. I don't want to burn up in the north country!"

"Did you see that deer? Or maybe it was a raccoon!"

By the time we crossed the Wahpeton/Breckenridge city limits, we had decided it wise to stop and pick up entertainment. Though a joint decision, I knew that in order to stay sane, we would need something beyond our conversation to pass the time.

Lunch in town was an extended affair, stretching beyond our standard cup of rice to include the local ice cream parlor and a fast-food joint. In between said treats, we hitchhiked to Wal-Mart to buy a couple of games, books, and Sudoku puzzles. We were convinced that with all of our extra free time, lounging in the front of the canoe with puzzles and games would be splendid. Somehow a bag of chips even made it into our cart, and it would have been rude to the cashier to do anything but purchase it.

Back at the confluence, Colton and I carried our bag of food and fun down the grassy slope to our poorly hidden canoe. In the months leading up to our trip, we had researched and worried about leaving the canoe unmonitored near towns. By now, we were accustomed to the generosity of locals and had become a little too trusting of their unwillingness to pillage our outfit. Once again, though, our canoe sat in the same spot we left it, beneath the river bridge that connected our home state to North Dakota. People are more honest than we gave them credit for.

In Minnesota, it is a standard pastime to take shots at North Dakota and its treeless, hill-less, windblown wasteland, perhaps if only because we know deep down that the rest of the nation likely thinks of Minnesota in a similar light. At this border, I will be the first to admit that the difference was quite indistinct. To the Minnesota side, looking up the Otter Tail River into the town of Breckenridge, was a riverside park filled with the tan of a muddy spring. The green tips of new grass spotted the hill up to the road, bits of life diffusing its way through the landmine of winterkill. Across the river into Wahpeton was equally brown, with a dense patch of leafless trees down to the water. To our north was the unmistakable mud-lined Red River, pointing the way to Canada and pine country.

Swish, swash, swish, swash, swish.

My eyes opened to the enveloping darkness inside my sleeping bag. I noticed right away that our canoe was heaving back and forth at a vastly greater frequency than normal. The water below the gunnels splashed turbulently, reminding me of the waves from Lac Qui Parle. There were many times on our trip when I woke up from a deep slumber, unaware of my surroundings, but not this time. I knew for certain that I was lying on the wet floor of the canoe's bow.

I pulled my head out of the sleeping bag to investigate the cause of our jerking vessel. During our afternoon snack break, we had temporarily removed the front seat, allowing more space in the bow to lie down. As I spun in our new bunk to face the back, I found Colton, paddling with all his might.

"We being chased?"

Colton shook his head. "I realized after you went to sleep that if we keep going at this rate, we could be to Lake Winnipeg in only a couple of days."

I nodded my head, understanding his reasoning for the sudden burst of energy. Colton had always been a go-getter. With a destination in mind, his goal was to reach that destination as fast as possible, pushing the limits of mind and body. He had the heart of a triathlete, and while I respected that, my interests continued to lie in the adventure. Some may call my take laziness, but I was in no hurry to leave nature behind and re-enter the city life back home. We had been planning the trip for years with adventure as our driving force, and it would continue to be that way. In the end, it was a good thing Colton had that drive to finish, or we might have taken until the next winter to reach our goal.

"Just be sure to pace yourself," I said.

He nodded back, set down his paddle, and then took a long swig of water from the red Nalgene water bottle that he pulled from the muddy floor. Tossing the bottle back to its puddle, he resumed the same ambitious pace.

"How did you sleep?" he asked between stinted breaths.

"I'm not sure if that qualified as sleep," I said, feeling the bottom of my sleeping bag. A puddle had formed beneath my rear end, soaking the bottom half of the material. "I'm also not sure that the waterproof sacks we made are actually waterproof."

Back in Granite Falls, the night that we slept on the concrete floor of the pavilion, we made use of the light from our bonfire to create "waterproof" sleeping bag covers. These covers were, in essence, heavy-duty garbage bags, duct-taped together to form a long enough tube to fit our sleeping bags. In theory, the cover *was* waterproof, but we hadn't considered that it would also keep water in the bag, if and when it found a way to enter.

"Really?" said Colton. "Mine seemed to work fine earlier."

"Well, mine clearly didn't." I took the sleeping bag out of the waterproof lining, hoping to help it dry. It looked to be a cloudless night, so I wasn't worried about rainfall.

"What time is it?" I asked, awaiting my looming night shift.

"About 8:30," said Colton, looking at the watch wrapped around the back thwart. "Wanna stop and have a quick dinner, then you can catch some Z's before we switch?"

"Sure."

After a cold chicken burrito on shore, I climbed into the bow and snuggled back in my sleeping bag. It was nearly impossible to sleep in the tight and persistently wet quarters, especially after the sun dropped below the tree line, taking the temperature with it. By the time 1:00 AM finally rolled around, my extremities were frozen and ready for the warmth of paddling. In my estimation, I slept deeply for no more than an hour or two all evening.

It was pitch black both inside and out of the sleeping bag now, and I struggled to find the flashlight resting near my head as I emerged. Colton claimed his eyes had adjusted, which explained why the light wasn't already in use.

"If we use it too much, we'll drain the batteries too fast," he added while pulling over to the muddy shore and stepping out carefully.

"Well," I said, grabbing hold of the flashlight with one hand and holding on to the side of the canoe with the other as I clambered out, "I may need it to read the map at least. Any idea where we are now?"

Colton spread out the map on the pack in front of the back seat while I shined the light on it from shore. He pointed to a location roughly between somewhere and nowhere.

"Okay." I looked ahead on the map for any bridges or dams that might be useful landmarks. "It looks like there's a bridge just past Wolverton that will warn us of a dam not long after. We'll have to portage around that."

"Sounds good," said Colton. Wasting no time at all, he jumped into the bow and crawled into his own bag, hopefully drier than mine. "Wake me when we get there, eh?"

I heard the zipper close around him and, just like that, I was alone.

The flashlight shined ahead, illuminating only a beam of light into an empty and silent darkness. Pointing it to my right and left lit only a tiny circle of brush atop the riverbank. Not only would using the light drain its battery, but it appeared to be of little use anyhow.

Looking up, I hoped to see a sky lit full with bright stars and a full moon. Clouds must have rolled in between dinner and now, because I could see neither. Turning off the flashlight, I held on to shore from the canoe for a while longer to give my eyes time to acclimate. While waiting, I put my hands in front of my face to test how far my vision could reach. Initially, six inches was the limit, but after five minutes, I could comfortably see the front of the canoe, enough for me to justify proceeding into the black abyss.

Despite the relatively comfortable confines of Minnesota and North Dakota, I have never felt more disoriented. Overall, sure, I knew where I was, but the blanket of darkness surrounding me was suffocating. River bends were impossible to predict until only feet from ramming headfirst into shore. Every movement or noise on the banks startled me as my imagination ran wild over what, or who, could be lurking beyond the shadows.

Our portable radio wasn't picking up a signal, so the minutes moved by like hours, and the hours like days. To pass time, I counted. For a while, counting up by ones to one hundred kept me awake, but eventually, I progressed to counting backwards, or by threes. Soon enough, I was doing long division in my head… or at least attempting to.

Several hours after starting my shift, I noticed a distant noise begin to permeate the black night as I wound my way north. At first, it was difficult to make out, but eventually, as the noise grew louder and closer, I recognized it to be music. *Was there a party going on out here?* I hoped that we wouldn't happen across drunk college kids relieving themselves in the already formidable water.

Rounding a bend, a picturesque farmhouse came into view on the North Dakota shore, sitting atop a gently sloping hillside. Every window in the house was illuminated, though no movement could be observed. I realized there could be no party taking place. The music escaping the home was that of an opera, and I immediately found myself within a horror film.

Reaching for the watch, I pushed the button to ignite its screen. 3:30 AM. Not a soul moved inside the home. As my mind raced, considering the most effective weapons on hand, my paddling strokes grew rapid and stealthy.

Would my paddle do enough damage? The fading scab on my finger from our unsuccessful carp hunt indicated it would not.

How about the flashlight? Although I don't want to ruin it. Our bear spray is tucked away somewhere... this is almost as deadly as a polar bear, right? Colton would understand using it in this sort of situation. I settled on the latter. Without wasting time, I tore into our survival bag and found the spray buried at the bottom.

As luck would have it, the farmhouse rested at the end of a peninsula, on another one of the river's classic horseshoe bends, forcing us to travel 270 degrees around the property before finally passing it. Every stump or tree on the North Dakota shore looked astonishingly like a human body, waiting for unsuspecting travelers to pass by in the middle of the night. The bear spray was cocked and loaded, safety off, and ready to go.

And with that, just as gradually as the music had grown, it also faded into the night. In the dawn hours, I told Colton about my harrowing tale, and though he needed some convincing, I'm sure the tremor in my voice helped reveal my genuine fear. In fact, most people found the story farfetched, but I maintain that it was *not* a hallucination and that I was truly lucky to escape that farmhouse alive.

Not long after the opera house, we passed under a monstrous steel bridge crossing the river. The sky was still inky, allowing the structure to startle me more than it should have. I knew that it would be coming eventually, but there was something ominous about slipping under the vacant bridge in the middle of the night, like it required my silence to pass through unharmed.

Knowing that a low-head dam was just ahead, I called to Colton. Dams on the Minnesota River were mostly powerful beasts, full of protective barriers and drops of ten to fifty feet. On the Red River, however, low-head dams were far less ferocious, typically dropping three to five feet, often with a gradual slope after the initial ledge. While the force on the Red River was less, the dangers of the dams were deceptively enhanced. They were often unmarked in person and lacked any protective barriers, yet fell severely enough that if an unsuspecting canoeist were to go in, they would emerge a tangled wreck. Indeed, back in Wahpeton, we had come close to paddling right over one in broad daylight, having unknowingly approached the lurking beast. After scrambling frantically towards shore at the last minute, a pair of young local fisherman came to our aid just before the ledge.

We waited in silence as Colton shined the flashlight ahead, searching for the upcoming dam. Upon finally reaching it, we pulled ashore and tossed out our loose gear. Next, I hopped off, allowing Colton, still half asleep, to hand me the remaining luggage. Once empty, Colton stepped out of the canoe to join me on shore. The bank was steeper than most and covered in mud, so as Colton stepped out, his foot slipped, sliding entirely into the icy river.

I stood paralyzed. Neck down, Colton was submerged in the river, and the temperature outside was no more than forty-five degrees. My mind and body felt numb from shock, and then I realized that my numbness would be nothing compared to what Colton's must have been. I immediately came to and grabbed a paddle beside me, reaching it out to Colton. The first reach was unsuccessful, his stiffening hand unable to grip the wet Kevlar surface. My mind raced and stood still all at once, unable to comprehend what was happening. As I hesitated, Colton's hand found a root on shore, and he was able to pull himself out of the water on his own. Partially up the bank, I reached out and dragged him the rest of the way. He looked at me and shivered as he said something inaudible. Even in the dark, I could see his lips quiver and fade to a lifeless purple.

"Space blanket," I finally heard him mutter.

In the survival pack before our first canoe trip, two years prior on the St. Croix River, we had tucked away a pair of silver blanket sheets that packed down to the size of a fist. I knew they were basically paper-thin sleeping bags that trapped a person's body heat inside, hopefully preventing hypothermia. Fortunately, though we had been close at times, I had never seen the things in use. In the early hours of this cold morning, the decision to end that streak came easy. Setting the tent up in record time, I nervously watched hypothermia-induced sleep take Colton.

CHAPTER 7

Canada Calls

Five hours after retrieving Colton from the Red River, we awoke to a warm morning inside our tent. Colton lay naked in his space blanket, layered too, with his sleeping bag. Outside the tent, Colton's soaked clothes and the rest of our gear sat strewn about at the edge of the river. Beyond the bank was the low-head dam that had stemmed our mid-night excursion. We hadn't planned on sleeping there, merely warming up, but we should have predicted that it would be impossible to stay awake in the warm confines of our beloved abode.

Both of us now pleasantly refreshed, and Colton assuredly not hypothermic, we continued on our way. For much of the morning, Colton mentally recovered by lounging in the front while I finished up my abbreviated shift. By lunchtime, he grew bored and joined in on the paddling.

Although we had been "entering" Fargo for over a day, the windiness of the Red River teased us into thinking that we were closer than we actually were. The houses that sparsely lined the banks of the river grew more common, but every time we thought we reached the city limits, signs of civilization disappeared and trees covered the shores once more. Our map was difficult to read, as every river bend looked identical both on paper and in person.

On one river bend, we noticed the houses and their backyards reach right up to the North Dakota bank. The homes were beautiful, and since it was approaching dinnertime, the thought of a home-cooked meal made my mouth water. Our mood was light, and we joked about stopping at one of the houses to invite ourselves inside. As we laughed, a woman hanging laundry in one such yard stopped and stared as we paddled by. The house was situated along a peninsula, with the river doubling back around itself. Initially, we took her to be yet another one of the many gawkers that we had encountered along the way, but when she reemerged on the far side of the peninsula five minutes later, she greeted us with a wave.

"Are you Colton and Sean?" she called out.

"That's us," we said back. Another fan, we presumed. Perhaps the local paper had already run a story about us.

"My husband works with somebody who knows someone who works with Colton's mom. We've been asked to intercept you on your way through and give you a ride into town to re-supply."

My mind was still on opera-singing axe-murderers from the night before, so her story seemed a bit sketchy to me. Just as I was about to remark that neither of our parents had told us about this pit stop, she played her trump card.

"We're sitting down for spaghetti in about fifteen minutes. You're free to join us!"

… She had us.

As it would turn out, the Johnson family was indeed a friend of a friend of a friend to the Wittes, and they also made a delicious spaghetti. We took the opportunity of an evening off to run into Fargo for a re-supply and to recuperate from the night before. Boy, did this city paddling spoil us. Part of me worried that we would be unprepared, softened, for the harsh reality of wilderness in the north. But then the other part of me had a full stomach, dry socks, wonderful hosts, and a quality night's sleep. To no surprise, comfort won out.

In order to make up for our adventurers' sin, we started bright and early the next morning. Less than thirty minutes into our day, we located yet another low-head dam; the first of three that we would pass in the Fargo-Moorhead area. There was a landing on the top and bottom of the dam for those who were wise enough to portage, but upon careful examination from shore, and a few prayers to the heavens, we declared it safe to run. The drop of the water pouring over the dam seemed tall, maybe three feet, but we couldn't see any visible rocks or obstructions, and we were looking for excitement.

Before making the plunge, we tied down the luggage and strapped our waterproof camera to the bow, setting it to record a video of our shenanigans. Typically, rapids and dams are run to save the time and the energy consumed during a portage. Clearly this was not our main concern, having spent double the time it would have taken to portage through just our scouting and preparation.

As we approached the drop, it became clear we had made a grave mistake. The place we were to presumably land at the bottom of the dam was too far over the ledge to see, and the preceding waves were monstrous. I was in the back, Colton in the front, my heart skipping beats. We were less than ten feet away when Colton yelled in mixed excitement and fear. There was no turning back; our only option now was to paddle hard and keep the craft pointed straight.

Landing at the bottom of the drop, the sharply pointed nose of our canoe sliced through the waves, scooping the gunnels below the surface and filling our canoe with water. Waves crashed in at all angles, soaking our outfit as we jerked violently up, down, and all around. The ordeal didn't last long, but by the time it was through, our lower halves were submerged in water, the canoe about an inch from having sunk completely. When freeboard, the distance between the water-surface and top of the canoe, is as small as it was at this moment, even the most miniscule movement would tip us. The added water made the canoe too heavy. Slowly but surely, we made our way to shore near the lower boat landing, where we emptied our load and dumped out the water. As we unloaded and reloaded, we stared at immaculate homes just on the other side of trees, reminding us once again how close our adventure was to a soft couch and flat-screen television. The comfort continued to beckon us, but the whispers of the north-flowing river were more enticing.

As we traveled deeper into the city of Fargo, parks beside the river grew more abundant. Along with the parks came fishermen and outdoor admirers, which meant more gawkers. Now more than ever, we received the longest stares. I could hardly blame them. We were a pair of scruffy young men paddling down the Red River, our canoe packed to the brim, and stickers explaining our actual route. Most strangely of all, only one of us was paddling while the other lounged up front, his back to the bow like a king, staring at the paddler like he was the king's chauffeur. If others didn't find the scene amusing, at least we did.

At the mid-town dam, the largest in Fargo, we were met by a reporter and his photographer taking pictures of our arrival. Taking quick notice, Colton sat up on the front thwart. The article this reporter wrote was eventually purchased by the Associated Press and subsequently distributed to newspapers worldwide. Hiking the several-hundred-yard portage around the dam, the reporter and photographer followed us, asking questions and shooting more pictures.

Just north of town at the next dam, two more newsmen with video cameras interviewed us while we ate lunch and prepared to switch between shifts. Colton would paddle for the next twelve hours, and it was my turn to finally lounge again. Over the next few miles, the camera crew traveled to different bridges and scenic overlooks on the river, catching shots of Colton paddling hard while I lazed in the front. We cackled to each other at the thought of how this would appear on the news. I cared little of how I would come across, comfortably reading in the bow while Colton paddled arduously. The sun was shining, the wind was calm, and there wasn't another dam for one hundred fifty miles. Clear sailing ahead!

The feeling in my fingers drifted away, leaving a tingly sensation that made it difficult to grip a paddle. Even with the extreme cold and unbearable aloneness, I felt myself drifting away, inching closer into sleep. What more could be expected, though, while paddling at four o'clock in the morning in the middle of farmland somewhere between Fargo and Grand Forks? Turning on the portable radio and listening to late night music helped for maybe ten minutes before I found myself again with eyes closed, my body on its way towards tipping into the river. Snapping back awake, I jumped sideways in fright and lost grip of my slippery paddle.

It made one echoing bang off the gunnel, then split the silent night with a slap like a beaver tail on the river's surface, before sliding the rest of the way into the water. Our momentum carried the craft past the paddle, its distance from me growing by the moment. I spun to my belly and crawled out over the stern's tip, swinging my arm towards the runaway oar in a last-ditch effort at recovery. It worked. Freezing water splashed about, jolting me awake and, ironically, warming my lifeless fingertips by a wave of exhilaration. I grasped the paddle and pulled it back in. Adrenaline pumped through me, and the shocking noise and temperature, coupled with having almost lost my most beloved tool kept me awake as the morning sun peaked over the eastern horizon.

At 5:30 AM, the local radio morning shows began, and I was at last in control of my wakefulness. By 7:00, the sun had fully risen, gradually thawing my hands as the air grew warmer. Next to a bridge that led to the farm town of Perley, Minnesota, I pulled into a landing and woke Colton up for breakfast. As we moseyed out of the canoe, I heard our names called over the radio.

"Colton, hold on! Listen!" I yelled.

The typical description was given. "Two eighteen-year-old boys from the Twin Cities are paddling through the area on their way to Hudson Bay. The trip in total is 2,200 miles and they have been paddling through the night since reaching the Red River." It wasn't until the end of their short segment about us that they mentioned a certain made-up complaint of Colton's. Of course, it was fabricated entirely in jest, but the look of disbelief on Colton's face was priceless. I doubt that I have ever laughed harder. It did make us wonder, what else was the media saying about us that we didn't know? Only by pure chance did we happen to hear this bit.

After calming down, we realized that we still couldn't feel our hands or feet, so a warm up was in order. A mile-long hike into Perley's sole gas station did the trick. We ignored the stares and bought a muffin, banana, and hot chocolate each. I wondered now how many of the stares were a result of stories made up by the media. As we sat down at a table inside, a few men approached us and shook our hands. They had read about us in the Fargo newspaper and, to our delight, did not hear the radio show this morning. We noticed a conspicuous picture of us on the front page of the paper that everybody was reading, and our minds were eased that this must be the source of their stares. One of the men was even kind enough to offer us a ride back to the river, and on the way, he told us of his travels on Lake Winnipeg years back. He and his friends were stranded on an island for a week, forced to survive the wrath of the treacherous lake. After assuring him we would be careful on the big water, he dropped us off and we were on our way.

The shifts were really beginning to take their toll. Because of an awful wind from the north, along with a distinct lack of trees in the area, the both of our paddling muscles were needed to make worthy progress, and we spent the morning canoeing together again. By 11:00 AM, the wind grew so fierce that paddling, even with our combined strength, was no longer worth the energy. We pulled into a drainage ditch on the North Dakota side to rest, which provided ample shelter while we waited for the wind to subside. After jumping across a patch of Red River mud, which had been known to be able to sink an average adult up to their knees, I lay down halfway up the grassy ditch to avoid the blustering gusts.

Dodging the Red River mud, so well-known for its infamous thickness and unforgiving suction force, was perhaps the biggest advantage to paddling through the night. Every time we avoided making camp, we also avoided the mud. At one point while stepping on shore for a break, my high-ankle hiking boots, aggressively tied to keep their waterproof nature alive, got so stuck in the cursed mud that I was sure my foot was trapped forever. As a child on the playground, we used to play a game called "quicksand," where certain areas of the ground threatened to suck you under if you remained stationary too long. It was always assumed that this game was practical training, for we were certain to encounter quicksand out in the world once we were big. And though that assumption never came fully to fruition, I'm confident that my practice in navigating the imaginary version paid off during my time on the Red River, successfully managing muck that was as close to real quicksand as most would ever get.

Once lying safely on the bank out of muds-way, it didn't take long for my mind to shut down, having had the last few days blend together in a blur of mediocre sleep and shift paddling. I'm sure that I dreamt, but I was so tired that I couldn't distinguish dream from reality. The real world felt like a dream, and my sleep was so deep that real dreams seemed to elude me. Two hours later, my eyes opened again, but I felt groggier than before.

Scanning the ground around my grassy bed, I searched for my hat with increasing panic. I was sure that I had set it beneath me as a pillow, but now my head's most trusted companion during the sub-freezing nights was missing. Eventually succumbing to the fact that it had blown away in the heavy wind, I cursed dramatically and agreed to move on. A new hat would have to wait until Winnipeg.

The wind had subsided only slightly, so for the remainder of the day, we paddled together. Colton was upset, hoping to continue paddling through the night to make faster progress, but it was clear that the shifts were destroying us, both mentally and physically. With warmer nights, perhaps this plan would have worked. As a final straw, we had heard reports from anglers at the gas station in Perley that ice remained on parts of Lake Winnipeg, so we knew in our guts that slowing down was the wisest option.

Although we were still paddling through spring melt, the rising Red River was far from its highest crest in history. In 1950 and 1997, the river rose to record levels, damaging the major cities along its banks and leaving the homes, farms, and villages in between isolated or destroyed. Other floods, notably during the 1960s and 1970s, had also plagued the region. In 2008, captives of the floods remained trapped in the banks. Bones from cows and deer stuck out of the mud like an excavated graveyard. Cars from the 1950s were particularly prominent victims, molded into shore with as little as hidden bumpers or as much as entire frames visible above ground. Sometimes trees grew through the cars' exteriors, or root systems developed fully within. By definition, the cars were a form of littering, but in practice, they had become a part of the river valley's environment. The spectacle was as fascinating as it was depressing.

Camping just above a dam in downtown Grand Forks, I basked in the simple joy of sleeping on solid ground. While I drifted off to sleep, Colton took advantage of the rare cell phone service and called his mom. She gave him the news that the article published by the Fargo newspaper had been bought out by the Associated Press and therefore, had gone international. I only partially heard him relay the information to me; my ears were in the tent, sheltered beneath an expansive grove of oak trees, but my mind was already dreaming peacefully of the lazy river ahead, paddling comfortably once again with each of us at the reins.

Drayton, North Dakota, one of the more prominent catfishing towns on the Red River, lies nestled away near a rocky dam, only miles from the Canadian border. During lunch near town, Colton turned his phone on and there was, among dozens of other voicemails, a message from Nick Coleman, the reporter with the Minneapolis *Star Tribune*, requesting a call. It had been some time since we had last spoken with Nick, and a lot had happened. From the way he put it, we were shocking everybody from home. In the beginning, between the weather, current, and illness, it appeared that we were soon to be one of the many who attempted, but failed to finish, this outrageous journey. Now we were exceeding expectations, turning disbelievers to believers... and back to disbelievers again. A small faction from back home was now convinced that we must be cheating – perhaps carrying a motor of some sort! Of course, all we could do was laugh along.

Only a mile or two past town, we came upon the Drayton Dam with a sign and lantern, warning us of the falls ahead in case we were still paddling by night. It was heartening to know that people were looking out for us this far from home. As it turned out, it was a good thing we hadn't attempted to pass over the dam at night, for the rocks surrounding it were as slippery as ice. Even in the bright afternoon sun, we must have fallen ten times each in the one-hundred-foot portage. Our struggles and several near broken ankles came much to the amusement of the countless fishermen below the dam. We laughed it off, knowing genuinely how foolish we must have looked.

Nearing the end of our afternoon, two fishermen in a motorboat approached our canoe. As it so happened, they were the same two who set out the lantern and sign in Drayton. They provided us a set of cool drinks, which soothed not only our parched throats but our drained minds after a day of sweaty paddling. Through the drinks and handfuls of fresh fruit (grapes weren't what we had in mind for a pit stop, but they appeased the taste buds refreshingly) the two told us a story of one of their brothers battling cancer. He had taken a strong interest in our trip and asked them to deliver a sticker for our canoe. It read "Failure is Not an Option" and was his motto. We accepted the addition to our craft with honor and promised to pay homage to the phrase whenever the going would get tough. Before departing, we autographed three of their paddles and passed along our best wishes to the brother.

It was tempting, after the pause we had taken, to call it a night and set up camp, but we pressed on. Not long after, we passed two men in lawn chairs at the top of a tall bank sitting with rifles, shooting at cans they had placed across the river. They invited us up for a drink, but we refused politely, unsure of how much they had already drunk, or their typical response to a declined party invitation. Plus, there were several hours left of daylight, and our camp this night would be the last on American soil. We could smell the fine Canadian air!

It had occurred to us during the long days of paddling that we might one day write a book about our travels. If you had asked us what the book's title would be as we neared the Canadian border, we would have answered, "*A Strong Wind from the North.*" The United States of America was doing her best to hold us within her grasp, to keep us safe from the untamed wilderness that we knew was ahead. On this day, though, nothing could hold us back; Canada was calling, and its untamed wilderness was just what we craved. It wasn't the first time either of us had been to Canada, having traveled across the border every few years on our annual canoe trips. This time was different, though; it was a landmark. The Canadian border would be roughly the halfway mark in total miles from Chaska to York Factory.

By noon, at a point we decided was approximately the border (there is no border control, sign, or landmark of any form on the river), Colton and I pulled ashore. We hiked a mile across forest and farm to the freeway where the customs station between North Dakota and Manitoba was located. It was the Friday of Memorial Day weekend and there was a long line of vehicles waiting to cross the border. Laughing merrily, we zigzagged through the cars, dressed in our typical attire, sweats and long johns, amidst honks and jeers from their inhabitants. Knowing full well the honks were hostile, directed in frustration with the ease by which we cut to the front of the line, we waved back and smiled, hoping to show that our intentions held no ill will.

Inside the station, the border patrol agents seemed initially wary of our story. We explained the trip, and with a similar sentiment to what we would receive from most Canadian officials, all they wanted to know was "*why*?" Apparently, our response, "For the heck of it," was either sufficient or stupid enough for their liking. Upon validating our story via the website Colton's mom put together, they let us through.

The next step was to retrieve some sort of map, however rudimentary it might be, to use between the border and Lake Winnipeg. Our Canadian-government-issued topographical maps started at the south end of the lake, and a simple road map would suffice for the one hundred fifty river-miles until then. Conveniently, a half of a mile down the road into Canada was a visitor center that had just the ticket. On our way there, we passed a road sign indicating a speed limit of 110. Images of speed-crazed Canucks littered my mind, and I wondered if we should be walking a few extra steps off the road. Before long, we realized that of course, in Canada, they used the metric system, so 110 signified the near equivalent of seventy miles per hour. We switched our watches to Celsius and brushed up on our metric conversion rates, scraping together memories from our sixth-grade math lessons. By the time we were hiking back to the border, we found ourselves scoffing at the imperial system and those "Yankees" who used it.

Passing the crossing stations on the way back to our canoe, Manitoba roadmaps in hand, it dawned on me how trusting the officers were once having learned what we were up to. A few months prior, Colton and I, along with a third friend, took a road-trip to Winnipeg to check out the city, scout the big lake, and buy our topographical maps. Of course, we could have bought the maps online and gotten the scouting done from pictures and stories, but a road-trip to Canada for three eighteen-year-olds was tough to pass up! When we had traveled into Manitoba at the very same border station back in March, the officials saw three teenagers in the middle of night, crossing for no good reason, so they searched our vehicle thoroughly. This time, they didn't even bother to peek in our packs.

"Freeze!" barked a deep voice from behind us, snapping me out of my daydream. Perhaps they had changed their minds and would check out the canoe after all.

We turned around, unsure of whether or not this situation warranted our hands to be raised. Two Canadian officials had come out of the building nearest us with their guns drawn. One of them, a sturdily built gentleman who seemed to be the superior in rank and age, stepped towards us.

"Where do you two think you're going?" the man demanded.

"Back to our canoe… you just approved us to cross!"

"No we didn't." He was sure of it.

It dawned on us that we were passing a different building from the one we had checked in through. This appeared to be a commercial station, serving semi-tractor trailers.

"We were at the other office," I said, my voice shaking.

The official looked at us a moment, then nodded to his partner. The younger man pulled a radio from his back pocket and made a call. The wait seemed to take minutes, hours even, and my heartbeat became so rapid I was sure it could be seen through my fleece sweater. Finally, the radio responded with a confirmation that we were, indeed, not illegally sneaking into the United States, breaking one of the more closely guarded laws of the land.

"You boys be safe up there, eh? That Lake Winnipeg can be a monster," he said, lowering his weapon. His Canadian accent was severe, sounding similar to the way most Americans believe Minnesotans speak. We thanked the officers and assured them that we would be safe, just as we had with countless others before.

Back at the canoe, Colton attempted to phone his mother to set up a rendezvous point where they would pick us up for the upcoming layover day. Winnipeg, our planned layover location, was still over a full day's paddle away, but we knew our parents would be crossing the border just hours behind us, so getting in contact with them was vital. Of course, cell reception failed us, and we were forced to leave our plans up to chance. After all, what's an adventure without some chance?

The day, quite typical for our spring, had warmed dramatically since morning, leaving us scorched beneath the newly Canadian sun. After weeks of paddling bare-chested, we were thoroughly sun-kissed, beyond the point of burning. Our Nalgene water bottles rolled around the bottom of our canoe, baking under the relentless sun. What I would have done for a handful of ice cubes.

Within five minutes of arriving at a bridge near the village of Letellier, our parents in Colton's father's SUV rolled up. By chance, they had stopped by to catch a glimpse of the river. As surprised as we were that they found us, they met us both with a heartfelt embrace. This layover would be our last bout of true civilization, and the last time we would see our parents before reaching Hudson Bay, a fact that loomed in the back of our minds. It also meant a paradise-filled weekend complete with amenities ranging from comfortable beds, hot tubs, and showers, to full-course meals, blue jeans, and all the ice we could ever ask for.

While transferring our gear to the Witte's vehicle, a fumbled handoff between Colton's father and myself resulted in a dropped camera, its screen cracking lethally on the rocks. The waterproof digital camera that served us from New Ulm to Winnipeg had perished. For a moment, Colton's father and I traded blame, but eventually decided it was the rock's fault for being too sharp.

As we boarded the SUV to depart, Colton's mom let out a howl. "Whew! Let's get you two into a shower!" It had been five days since the shower at the Johnsons' in Fargo – short for our standards.

About to retort that I thought we smelled perfectly fine, Colton butted in.

"Gladly," he said. "Sean stinks!"

CHAPTER 8

This Was Why

Letellier is one of several small French communities scattered between the southern Manitoba border and Winnipeg. Aside from the thick French-Canadian accents with which the locals spoke, the clearest evidence of their background appeared on every road and building sign, each inscribed in both French and English.

On top of the riverbank at the Letellier Bridge, we met the Houle family, who had owned their riverside farm for generations. They allowed us to store our canoe and unneeded luggage in a shed and told us about their experience with a group of four college students in the 1970s who stayed at the Houle farm in the midst of completing nearly the same trip. The college kids were laid over for a couple of days due to record flooding throughout the region. One of them later wrote a book about their adventure and dedicated a full section to their time with the Houles. Their farm, it seemed, was a rite of passage for American canoeists.

Located fifty miles north of Letellier and just over sixty miles from the border, as the crow flies, the city of Winnipeg was our final layover location, this time for two nights. Winnipeg itself has a population of nearly 700,000 residents and is by far the largest settlement in Manitoba. Before European settlers arrived, its location served as a cultural hub due to the confluence of the two most prominent regional rivers: the Red and the Assiniboine. Its geographic significance, coupled with its close proximity to Lake Winnipeg to the north, served quite valuable for the fur traders of the region in the 18th and 19th centuries.

Before visiting, Colton and I were under the assumption that Winnipeg was a mid-sized northern city, not unlike Fargo. It was a surprise then to realize that Winnipeg today is nearly the size of Minneapolis and St. Paul combined (barring the surrounding Twin Cities suburbs). Because of this, we noted that when our parents were to drop us off in two days' time back at the Houle family farm, we would need to plan accordingly to avoid camping in the city limits. Sleeping along the riverbank in downtown Winnipeg seemed about as safe as camping with polar bears on the shores of Hudson Bay. That was a worry for after the layover, though, as our present concern lay solely with our first real meal in days. Attempting to appear cultured, we initially pushed for some form of French cuisine, but when the smell of hamburgers and fries wafted past our car window, we succumbed to our American roots and chose good ol' greasy fried food. At least the fries were French.

Saturday, the first full layover day, was spent running more errands than we had intended for our "day off." With the exception of a handful of small towns in the first hundred miles after Winnipeg, we would only pass through two Cree villages for the remaining distance to York Factory. The villages, Norway House and Oxford House, both between Lake Winnipeg and Hudson Bay, were extremely remote, so they would not be reliable stops for re-supplying on our necessities. Rumor had it a bottle of Coca-Cola ran upwards of ten dollars in Oxford House. I wasn't sure what the exchange rate was, but that seemed to price us out of the market for legitimate supplies or impromptu sweets.

Our supply of cold pizza from Montevideo was long gone, but the concept remained intriguing, so we made sure to add it to our supply list. A local pizza joint down the road had a special on extra-larges, so we ordered four and separated them into a dozen plastic baggies. Without a cooler, we were unsure of how long they would last but figured it was still cold enough at night to qualify as refrigeration.

For the first few hours of our day, we crouched around the bed in my parents' hotel room, which was conveniently nestled along the

Red River as it wound through the city. Colton and I stretched out the four maps that would take us from the start of Lake Winnipeg to Hudson Bay and estimated our projected progress for each day ahead. Accuracy was vital in order to ration correctly, for if a can of soda cost ten dollars, I didn't dare imagine what pre-cooked chicken packets would run in the Canadian bush.

Unfortunately, estimating progress on the tumultuous Lake Winnipeg was near impossible. We had heard from local experts that it could take anywhere from two weeks to two months to paddle, depending on weather. By this time, however, we had grown leery of most of the estimations locals would give us, having noticed their tendency to overestimate the difficulty of their own terrain. Instead, we used our typical daily lake distance of forty miles to predict travel. As a measure of caution, we included two extra days of rations in case of a weather layover.

From Norway House to York Factory and Hudson Bay there remained roughly five hundred miles of rivers, lakes, and rapids traveled by less than a dozen people per year. Our experience in real rapids was basically nil, and some of the lakes could be a challenge if the weather wasn't in our favor. Our most recent bit of intel from Oxford House, two hundred miles from York Factory, said that trucks were still driving on the lake-ice. It appeared there was a very real chance that we would catch back up with winter. In the end, we packed for thirty days of travel to reach Hudson Bay from Winnipeg. It could be less, but unless we wanted to go hungry, it couldn't be more.

At the Downtown Winnipeg train depot, we ordered tickets for the return trip. Colton's mom confirmed that we had received enough donation money to schedule a floatplane to pick us up from our destination. Once our route was complete, we planned to set off the SPOT Messenger and stay put. That way, our parents could communicate to the pilot our exact location. We would be flown from York Factory to Gillam, and then board the train for its twenty-four-hour ride back to Winnipeg. My father would be there to pick us up and drive us the rest of the way home. The plan was seamless!

After packing all afternoon in the hotel's third-floor hallway, interspersed with a radio and TV interview near the river for local stations, we were finally able to relax by the pool for the evening. Watching Colton's father go down the waterslide headfirst while the water hilariously turned off mid-ride (and thus sending him to a screeching halt), made us forget that in one day's time, we would be back on the muddy Red River, itching for another night of luxury. It was almost as though we were home again. In the end, I was glad that we spent only two nights in town, for many more and I doubt we would have been able to leave. The wilderness tugged at our heartstrings, but the longer we strayed, the weaker those strings grew.

Back at the Houle farm near Letellier, Colton and I refilled our Nalgenes and water jug one final time. The Minnesota and Red Rivers were too polluted for a filter to suffice, but Lake Winnipeg was large enough to dilute any in-flowing chemicals thoroughly enough, so a hand-pump filter was all we would need from there on out.

We were finally able to meet Diny Houle – the gentlemen who had, in his early twenties, hosted the crew of canoeists during the 1970s flood. Colton and I thanked him for storing our canoe in the shed, and he mentioned what a pleasure it was to lend a helping hand to another expedition group on their way to Hudson Bay.

"So how do you boys plan to tackle the big lake?" he asked, referring to Lake Winnipeg.

"We'll follow the west shore up until the narrows," said Colton, "then we'll hop over to the east side and take that shore until the end."

"Good plan!" said Diny. "How much time do you have set aside?"

"For the lake?" I responded. "Should be about ten days, accounting for weather."

A small smile crept onto Diny's face. We recognized it as the pity smile. "Sorry to burst your bubble there, fellas," he shook his head, "but we've seen trained military men take one or two months to paddle that lake."

I would say that we were used to the pity smile, and there is no doubt that we fully understood the magnitude of the task ahead, but the constant pessimism towards our abilities had grown disheartening. It wasn't Diny's fault. He was generous beyond measure and would never have discouraged us intentionally. In fact, he was doing just the opposite. Too many times paddlers had ventured out, underestimating nature and overestimating their abilities, and the results were typically catastrophic. His only wish was to warn us and hope that we would be realistic enough for our own well-being.

We gave Diny a nod and final thanks, and he bade us good luck. By the canoe, we hugged our parents one more time, as my mother handed me a goodbye present: a new winter hat, this one white. There were no tears, at least that we saw, for their faith in us had grown immensely, but the moment was somber nonetheless. We wouldn't see them again until we had succeeded. Failure was not an option.

Back on the Red River, roughly eighty river-miles south of Winnipeg, we were once again alone. It was a beautiful day to be paddling, despite the persistent north wind. Our prolonged goodbye prevented us from getting back on the water until after lunchtime, so our hope was to paddle hard and late, to make up as much ground as possible in the abbreviated day.

Within no time, the rested feeling from our layover vanished and it was like we had never left the water. One significant difference, though, was noticeable: a new canoe. Our Bell North Bay, the canoe that had treated us so well for the first 1,100 miles of our trip, was officially retired, strapped to the top of Colton's parents' SUV and suffering a long, humiliating ride back to Chaska.

The lightweight Kevlar canoe was perfect for flat water paddling and a true blessing while climbing the Minnesota River current. The shape of the nose, though, was too pointed to handle big waves and rough rapids, as we found out first hand with the dam in Fargo. A sharply pointed bow cuts through the water instead of riding over it, effectively submerging the nose of the vessel in even remotely rough water. Additionally, the material was fragile due to its light weight, and would be punctured easily if we hit a sharp rock in rapids.

Enter Bloomitte #2: A forest green Bell Alaskan. One foot shorter, a rounded nose, and made of Royalex, which would dent instead of puncture, the updated canoe was our new home. There was a bit of guilt at first, like we were cheating on the North Bay with a slightly slower, heavier, and sturdier canoe. Within an hour's use of her, though, we knew the trade would be for the best. The Alaskan turned on a dime and seemed unable to tip when we tried. Running rapids in her would be a cinch!

Atop our new vessel was a homemade spray skirt that our fathers put together out of black landscaping poly, duct tape, and Velcro. Acting as a cover, spray skirts prevent water from pouring over the sides and into an otherwise open canoe. Without one, heavy rapids or breaking waves could fill our canoe in a heartbeat, causing it to flip easier than the North Bay on its tippiest of circumstances. We had requested our parents to purchase a professionally manufactured one with our donation money, but apparently, the apple didn't fall far from the tree. Using the same materials Colton and I had for our "waterproof" sleeping bag covers, our fathers improvised.

One full day after our layover, still several river-miles south of Winnipeg, we stopped for lunch in the French settlement of St. Adolphus. Stretching our legs, we decided to take a walk around town. My hands, even after the day and a half layover, were cracked and bleeding from the constant exposure to mud and its subsequent drying. Sticking our hands in the river only made it worse, and the burning sensation was unbearable, so I was hell-bent on finding a lotion of some sort to let them heal. Naturally, none could be found, and the dust from the gravel road only made it worse.

Near a hidden diner in town, tucked away beneath a grove of dense pines, we met a man who owned a home on Lake Winnipeg. He gave us some advice about the marshy delta where the Red River flows into the lake, and then assured us that with proper motivation and prudent caution, we could paddle Lake Winnipeg. It was a breath of fresh air to hear somebody other than our parents say they believed in us.

On our way out of town, we stopped at a gas station to replace our ruined digital camera. This time, unable to afford a third digital (the first was ruined on Day 2), we opted for five disposable cameras, each double-layered within plastic baggies for custom-made waterproofing.

Approaching the city limits of Winnipeg had a different feel than Fargo, especially from our perspective on the river. American cities seemed to gradually build up from sparse homes and neighborhoods to larger, more frequent buildings, and then finally to the city-center. Winnipeg, however, seemed to sprout out from the fields in the matter of a single river bend. After paddling under the "Perimeter Highway," a freeway that circumnavigates the metropolis, we found ourselves abruptly within town. Night began to fall as we passed the University of Manitoba, and we suddenly realized that camping would be an issue. The city crept up faster than the sun went down, so that camping hadn't been in our thoughts. Consulting the map, we couldn't locate any parks within easy reach.

"We could stay under a bridge," I offered.

"That seems a bit dangerous," said Colton. He motioned ahead to the left bank. "Let's just pull over up here and hang out 'til it's dark, then pitch the tent and leave by dawn."

We weren't sure what the penalty in Canada was for illegal camping, but hoped they extradited if it included jail time. Even if they didn't, a Canadian prison seemed more desirable than staying in sleeping bags under the interstate. A twenty-foot row of trees stretched between the river on the left bank where Colton had motioned and some buildings beyond. As we drifted up to the water's edge, we spotted a bonfire not far down the shore. While unpacking, we considered checking it out, but a longhaired man on a bicycle approached from the same direction.

"You can't make fires in the city!" he said, meeting us at the bank.

"That wasn't us," Colton quipped back. "We thought it was *yours!*"

He stared inquisitively. I could safely say that he wasn't police, though I had heard stories about Canadian Mounties. Had they swapped their horses and hats for bicycles and hippie-hair?

I pointed back to our canoe resting upon shore. "We're just paddling through the city, heading north. It's almost dark, so we had to pull over and camp."

The man looked at us some more. He wore shorts that seemed too baggy for riding a bike, and his tie-dye shirt looked a bit disheveled.

"Well..." he said, taking another look at the fire downstream, "camping isn't allowed in the city-limits either, and I suspect that whoever made that fire is coming back, so I wouldn't suggest trying. I've got an apartment just down the road. Why don't you boys stay with me? Always like lending a hand to fellow travelers."

Colton and I looked at each other. Fellow travelers... he confirmed he wasn't a Mountie, but who were the "travelers" that he spoke of? Sleeping under a bridge seemed sketchy, but so did this. It didn't appear that we had many other options.

"Alright... thanks!" we said after a brief deliberation.

"Great. My name's David." His demeanor immediately changed. "I've got to go finish an errand. You boys had dinner yet?"

We shook our heads.

"The Pony Corral is right behind us here. Why don't you grab a table on the deck and I'll meet you in say, an hour?"

"Well, he seemed nice," I said to Colton as we walked up to the restaurant beyond the trees. Just then, we realized where we were. Next door to the Pony Corral was the hotel where we had stayed with our parents two nights before. We really were right in the city. Camping overnight could have been a nightmare.

David kept his word and arrived at the restaurant not long after we finished eating. He sat down, ordered us a round of cocktails, and told us his stories of traveling around North America. He took a keen interest in our trip and encouraged us to never give up on our adventurous spirit. While there were some unanswered questions surrounding David, it didn't take long for us to trust him.

Back at his apartment, we checked in using our SPOT Messenger and chuckled at the confusion that we must have caused our followers. Checking in from the balcony of a random apartment? That was surely not in our itinerary.

The night was spent sipping on various beverages that David concocted, each of us continuing to rehash travel stories. It occurred to me during our conversation that night that we were no longer the wide-eyed listeners that we had been only weeks prior back on Lac Qui Parle. Our stories went punch-for-punch with David's, and he was the first to admit it. Occasionally, David would leave for thirty minutes at a time to run more errands and trusted Colton and me to

This Was Why

hang out and chat alone in his home. During one prolonged absence, we finally slipped off into sleep.

Awaking at sunrise on David's living room floor, we packed up and decided it would be rude to leave without saying goodbye. We found David sleeping, fully clothed, on a sheet-less mattress in his bedroom. Not taking no for an answer, he demanded to treat us to breakfast across the street.

"Across the street" turned out to be the continental breakfast at the very hotel that we had stayed at during our layover. Twisting our consciences just slightly, we convinced ourselves eating there was fine, knowing that we had skipped one of our free meals there just a few days ago. The employees were unaware of our intrusion, but our guilt got the better of us. We slyly dropped a few American dollars on the table before leaving.

We departed on our journey through the remainder of the city, quickly deciding to aim for Lake Winnipeg by nightfall. On the north end of town, we saw the first paddlers since Mankato. Three kayakers paddled one river bend ahead of us during the chilly morning hours. They were presumably from the famous Winnipeg Paddling Club, given our proximity to its headquarters. We never did get close enough to chat with them, but it was heartening to see their presence, even from a distance.

We stopped for lunch in the town of Lockport, aptly named for the lock and dam in the center of town, which enables safe passage for boats and barges traveling between Winnipeg and the north country. Rounding a bend in the river, the lock sat at the end of a narrow channel, detached from the riverbed. To its right was the main flowage, directing a majority of the river down a powerful dam. Initially, we had expected to portage around this dam, but while eating lunch on the island between the waterways, we agreed to investigate the requirements for traveling down the lock. If we could avoid portaging over the busy road, or avoid portaging all together, for that matter, the inquiry would be worth it.

As luck would have it, we were visiting Lockport on the first day that the lock was open for the season. Even more fortunate, our seventeen-foot Bell Alaskan met the minimum boat length perfectly.

The operator seemed pleased to allow us passage, but still we felt a tad guilty paddling into the topside entrance of a contraption meant for seventy-foot barges. Emerging from the water next to the right wall, beside my position in the bow, was a thick rope. It measured several inches in diameter and stretched onto the ledge only a foot above the water's surface, where it connected to a metal pole.

"You're gonna want to hold on," the operator said to me, casually motioning towards the rope as he spit out his gum.

I grabbed on. How rapidly was the water going to drop if I was required to hold on? No sooner did the thought cross my mind before suddenly the rope was moving upward through my hand, and the ledge next to us began to rise.

"We're going down!"

It wasn't as fast as I feared, but my grip held tight on the rope nonetheless. We watched the walls surrounding us move upwards as the water we floated upon dropped. Just half of the way down, twenty feet, water could already be heard leaking through the seams of the upper doors. Looking back, arches of water spurted from the cracks like a stressed levee, the proverbial weight of the Red River behind it. I tried not to think about what would happen if the wall gave way.

Finally, forty feet below the top of the lock, the rope in my hand stopped. Water continued to drizzle through the fissures behind us, but the wall ahead was our sole focus. Like a castle gate, the wall-doors opened, inviting us northward into a vast kingdom.

Onward we paddled, bidding our lock-guide above a farewell wave. The bottom of the dam was littered with fishing boats, and we later learned that this location was one of the premier catfishing holes in the world. Just after the lock, the north end of a colossal diversion channel merged with the river. Created in the 1960s to avoid continued damage from the notorious Red River floods through Winnipeg, the canal surrounds the entire metropolitan region. Controversial during its construction, the residents of Winnipeg often view it today as a lifesaver, having successfully diverted dozens of floods from the city's limits.

The clear blue sky turned gradually orange to the west as the shores of the Red River transformed from woods and fields to marsh

and cattails. There were a handful of spots that looked high and dry
enough for pitching a tent, but the day was not over yet, and we
yearned for the big lake. Soon enough, though, those dry campsites
were few and far between.

Upon the advice from the man back in St. Adolphus, we took a
gamble and veered away from the main channel of the marshy river
delta. The detour brought us northwest into Netley Lake. On our
topographical maps, the shallow lake looked just deep enough to
cross. It was a short cut, mileage-wise, to be sure, but a risky one at
that. We would not reach new high ground until the north end, where
a tiny road appeared to separate Netley Lake from Lake Winnipeg. If
all went as planned, we would be camping on the southern shore of
Lake Winnipeg by nightfall.

Of course, evident from our experiences thus far, rarely does all
go as planned in the wild. Nature has its endearing ways of tricking
you into a false sense of security and then striking you down when
you least expect it. Our security on Netley Lake was caused by
perhaps the most beautiful sunset the human race has ever witnessed.
The orange sky reflected on the mirrored water, meeting flawlessly
at the horizon. We were paddling straight into Heaven.

SCREECH!

The canoe jolted to a stop. I looked down and found my paddle's
blade digging into the sandy bottom. So mesmerized by the horizon,
neither of us noticed as we entered into a shallow reef. Several weeds
stretched their tips above the lake's surface, but they were so slight
that we hadn't seen them until it was too late. Our canoe's bottom
was stuck in only inches of water. Looking around, it dawned on me
that we were darn near the center of the lake, miles from shore in any
direction. It didn't look good.

"What do we do?" I asked, perplexed.

"Nothing else we can do," said Colton. "Let's get out and push.
We've gotta reach the northern shore by dark."

Pushing the canoe was no easy task. The lake bottom was strong
enough to hold us up from paddling, but so soft that we sank to our
knees while standing. Losing our collective body-weight when we
got out was enough to float the canoe, but pushing it remained slow

going due to our ineffective walking conditions.

Daylight was diminishing quickly, but we thankfully reached a point a few hundred yards later where Colton and I could get back in the canoe and paddle. Racing to the northern shore, we surveyed the water in front of us, nervously expecting another bog. If we stalled again, I doubted we would make it to shore before dark.

Just when it seemed we would be in the clear, a far more obvious marsh appeared ahead. Cattails higher than our heads stretched in front of us, and the wall of weeds continued as far as we could see to our left and right. The maps had deceived us, as this marsh wasn't marked. There appeared to be no way either through or around, yet our goal of the north shore, and Lake Winnipeg beyond it, lay on the other side. We were stumped.

Night had finally fallen, and our problem would not be solved in the dark. We gave in to nature and decided to call it a day. Ramming the canoe through the perimeter of the marsh, we pushed in as far as we could muster. Once firmly stuck, we set out our buoyant gear on the cattails, rearranged our packs, and made camp in the boat.

As twilight passed into nighttime, the sky became a gorgeous backdrop for the Northern Lights. The Aurora Borealis danced upon a canopy of dense stars as we separately watched in awe from the canoe's floor. I felt I could reach up and snatch a constellation of my own. So far from artificial light, I've never felt so at peace. We were lost in a sea of weeds, facing an impending dilemma that had no apparent solution, but none of that mattered. The world seemed so vast, yet the sky so small, and the problems of the day disappeared with the realization that we put ourselves here. Finally, we found the answer to all those who questioned *why* we would attempt such an endeavor. This was why.

CHAPTER 9

An Inland Sea

When I awoke in the Bell Alaskan, surrounded by the weeds of Netley Lake, it took a moment to realize what lay ahead. The temperature had dropped substantially overnight, and cold dew glistened on our sleeping bags. The peace that I had felt before falling asleep, looking at the stars, was not completely gone, however, as silence engulfed the cool morning air.

I nudged Colton awake with my feet, and we nibbled on slices of cold pizza while contemplating our next move. Standing up in the canoe, I scanned the horizon for a daylight assessment of our options. Netley Lake stretched beyond my line of sight back to the south. It would be torturous to backtrack all that way. Not an option. To the east and west were miles more of cattails; another definite "no." Looking north, I saw, perhaps a mile away, pine trees marking high ground at the north end of the lake. Just beyond those trees, we knew was Lake Winnipeg.

I sat back down in the canoe and looked at Colton. He was finishing off his slice of pepperoni pizza and didn't look up.

"Well," I said, "we've really just got one choice. There's trees to the north, just like we thought. Probably the road that the map marks. We've just gotta get there."

Colton examined his crust for a moment, then nodded, clicking his cheek in resignation. "This won't be fun."

It wasn't. Unable to spare a set of dry clothes, we stripped our lower halves down to underwear, less our neoprene lining boots, and hopped in. The water might as well have been ice. My boots sank into the muddy bottom, just as they had the previous night in the middle of the lake. This time, however, the water was deeper, reaching past our waists and soaking the bottom of our fleece tops. Disturbing the mud and soil below released the terrible smell of swamp into the air, like the combination of an outhouse and sewage-water. Every step we made set loose more of the pungent toxins just beneath our noses.

Seeing as the weeds were thick enough for our canoe to rest solidly overnight, trying to move it any further was a chore. Colton stood behind the stern while I grasped the rope connected to the bow. With a heave-ho, we struggled forward with all our might. I fell the first go-around, but we moved forward four feet. Each step towards land was a hard earned success but added fresh scratch marks to our shins from the razor sharp weeds.

Eventually, the water grew shallow enough for us to both push the canoe from the sides, and our steps became more consistent. In a little more than an hour, the marsh became so shallow that our craft no longer floated, but instead rested upon the dry reeds above water. We could see the trees only a couple hundred yards away now, so with the packs on our back, we portaged the rest of the way to solid ground. This close, just a glimpse of the big lake would be enough to raise our spirits.

Finally to shore, we picked our way through a tangle of trees to a gravel road, on the other side of which sat a few small homes. I couldn't believe it. We had felt so alone out in that marsh, yet here was civilization, within shouting distance the entire time. Down the road to the right, we could see a clearing, and knew with certainty that this was our destination. As I rounded the curve to the opening, I could hear the sound of small waves splashing over a rocky shore. It was here. I set down my pack to grab the camera from my pocket. Pointing it forward, I took my first look at Lake Winnipeg.

Colton hadn't noticed my stalling to capture the moment, so he continued ahead and centered himself perfectly in my shot. His face shined in awe, no different from my own. I pushed the disposable camera's trigger and removed the viewfinder from my face. My stomach dropped. *We must be crazy.* Our destination of Norway

An Inland Sea

House on the north end of the lake was some two hundred fifty miles beyond the water-lined horizon. It was an inland sea.

To understand Lake Winnipeg paddling, one must first understand the geographic abnormalities that the lake displays. At nearly ten thousand square miles of surface area, Lake Winnipeg is the eleventh largest freshwater lake in the world. It spans two hundred fifty miles from the south to north end and, at its widest point, reaches nearly one hundred miles across. Looking at a map, the shape of the lake resembles a misshapen peanut shell, consisting of two basins, the Northern and the Southern. The Southern Basin is significantly smaller in size, but holds the vast majority of human activity, while the Northern Basin, much larger and deeper, is nearly uninhabited. Shockingly, with the exception of a short channel that connects the two basins, the lake's average depth is only twelve meters, less than forty feet.

There are countless shallow reefs stretching for hundreds of feet perpendicularly from shore, and its massive surface area creates wildly unpredictable weather. That combination ensures that, even on the most harmless of days, the possibility of sudden disaster must be vigilantly monitored. For weeks, we had heard folk tales of paddlers and anglers setting out on calm, sunny days, only for a storm to pop up unexpectedly, the boaters never to be heard from again. Treacherous reefs and nearly constant rolling waves make it often necessary to travel a mile away from shore, which cuts against almost every small-boat-on-big-water instinct. And, naturally, upon hearing that storms had the potential to roll up in a matter of minutes, being a mile from shore sounded like a death sentence.

So when we spent the majority of our first day in calm waters on Lake Winnipeg's western shore, scoffing at the alarmists in local towns, we knew in the back of our minds that it wouldn't last long. Only fools scoff at temporary signs of good fortune.

After passing the quaint town of Gimli, the eastern horizon across the lake faded into a dark shade of blue, and the low rumble of thunder threatened through the Canadian sky. Our hopes of reaching a park only miles ahead were thwarted. We raced to shore, following our plan to give the great lake its much-deserved heed. Rain began pattering our hoods as we pulled into a bare embankment. Just over the bank was a swamp, providing equally limited protection from impending winds. Down the shore, though, we spotted a mature cove of trees, bristling in the storm's front.

A flat, tree-protected, and grass-bottom site had the makings of the ultimate Lake Winnipeg campsite. That is until we found, nestled within mere feet from the edge of the forest, an expansive mansion. The brown siding blended perfectly with the woods behind it, and the windows radiated the darkness within. Our only hints that somebody might be home were two pickup trucks parked at the side of the house.

As Colton scrambled, setting the tent up before imminent downpour, I rang the doorbell, hoping to find someone that would grant us camping permission. Either they were all asleep or nobody was home, as no movement could be seen inside. Just in case, I wrote a quick note on a page from my journal explaining our circumstances and stuffed it between the doorjamb and front door.

By 6:00 AM the next morning, the storm had passed and the inhabitants of our host home had not yet awoken or were too afraid to approach us. In no position to wait around and find out, we got onto the water immediately, without as much as a backwards glance. We knew our Canadian neighbors to the north had a friendly reputation, but putting it to the test by trespassing wasn't on our shortlist of to-do's.

The storm overnight brought in a new wind from the north, creating something we had heard about the weekend before in Winnipeg – a funnel-like effect caused by the lake's unique shape. Like the grains of an overturned hourglass, the narrows connecting the two basins were rumored to hold a tide-like current in persistent winds, an effect of the lake attempting to push its nearly seventy cubic miles of water through the four-mile wide channel. This effect persisted for miles beyond the narrows, and we found ourselves on the Minnesota River again, this time fighting a north wind and breaking rollers in addition to the steady current.

As the Southern Basin reaches the narrows, the western shore turns to the east, pointing an enormous peninsula into the middle of the lake. We snuck to the south of the peninsula and north of Hecla Island, the biggest island on the lake, famous for a small town on its eastern edge and its accompanying golf course. Hidden from the wind, we enjoyed the momentarily peaceful water by singing duets of our favorite tunes. Along the mainland shore, we paddled calmly past clusters of cabins, most of which were quiet and still. Their emptiness was fortunate, as my singing voice wasn't exactly fit for public consumption.

Once the sun began to drop, so too did the temperature, and our t-shirts and gym shorts were no longer warm enough. On the dock of an empty cabin we climbed up and changed into pants and jackets, hoping cheerfully that nobody was home. Now finally able to filter our drinking water, we filled up our water bottles for the last leg of the night. It felt glorious to finally drink cold, fresh water. After departing from the dock, a four-mile crossing to the eastern shore of the lake stood ahead of us.

As we drifted out into the open sea, the sun set beautifully over the northwest skies. It was the second time in recent days that our evening finished with a picturesque view. I felt so fortunate to be here, but so small. The vastness of Lake Winnipeg and the land to the north was finally sinking in, and I couldn't help but feel like we were testing Mother Earth. Colton and I, in our tiny canoe, meant nothing to the unforgiving elements into which we paddled. We were climbers on an unstable mountain. Our goal of reaching the summit required hard work and determination, but if nature so wished, she could crush us in an instant with her storms, high winds, and hypothermic temperatures. Instead of avalanches and cliffs to fear, we had tsunami-sized waves and man-eating bears. I had never felt more powerless.

An unprotected twelve miles to the upper narrows, Loon Straits, through relentless waves and freezing wind was a disheartening start to our next day's paddle. The wind came from the north, like nature's attempt to test our wills before we made it any further. She wanted to ensure we were committed. As the rain poured down, freezing through our rain gear and gloves, the need to stop and break eventually took over. The wild north had reared her ugly head, and it made city boys like us cower.

On the western shore of the upper narrows was the town of Pine Dock, nestled neatly within a wind-protected cove. At least, according to the map, it was a town. Upon docking our boat at a large but empty boardwalk that appeared to be fit for ocean steamers, we hiked up a shallow hill into town, eager for cover. Suddenly, we found ourselves in the midst of a real life ghost town. The rain had calmed slightly, giving way to a misty fog that blanketed our surroundings in a dense sea of grey. Not a soul was in sight, and I could hear my heart pounding, rising with each step we took further into town. The soft mist pattered onto the hood of my raincoat, eventually muffling my heartbeat to a muted thud.

In the distance, we spotted a glimpse of movement, or perhaps just a shadow. Our eyes peeled for any sign of life through the sparse homes, all of which were run-down in the same sort of way, from a lifetime of underuse. The door to an old phone booth sat ajar on the right side of the road with its phone swaying coldly, hung from its metal cord. As I approached the phone to investigate, Colton spotted a single inhabited house down the road, given away by the peacefully billowing smoke coming from its chimney.

"Do we check it out?" he asked.

All we really wanted was a warm break – anything to escape from our wet gloom. It didn't take more than a moment for me to nod in the affirmative, if nothing else to ask where we might seek refuge for our lunch. As we neared the home, the sweet smell of burning cedar reached our noses, and the uneasiness I previously felt vanished. It reminded me of the campfires we made during our trips to the Boundary Waters. At night, Colton's dad would tell long jokes and play James Taylor tunes on his acoustic guitar while the rest of us ate s'mores and watched the heavens in awe. It was home, and this smell brought me back there.

Colton knocked on the door after a brief debate about who should do so, and a man who must have been nearly ninety years old answered, claiming to have heard about us on the Winnipeg news station. Upon being asked about some shelter, the man and his wife graciously offered to treat us to a warm meal.

During our time in Pine Dock, we heard stories about the area's history. Some seemed true, and some sounded much more like old wives' tales – stories of the sea and long-lost sailors. Despite being what used to be a somewhat thriving city, Pine Dock had been virtually abandoned in recent years. Nearby was a fly-in fishing resort, but the tourists from there rarely made the trip into town. One possible factor in its abandonment was a recent wolf infestation. Unsure of exactly what sparked it, the wolves had grown more and more hostile in recent years, venturing into town and attacking innocent civilians. After that, the stories shifted into urban legend, though their origin, stemming from aggressive wolves, appeared to be genuine.

During lunch, the mist turned into a downpour; heavy, penny-sized droplets pounded the tin roof, hammering our already low esteem yet further. According to the news, the remainder of the day would be wet, and the next day would be defined by an even stronger wind from the north. Weighing our options, either wasting the day inside or continuing on through the surge of rain, we concluded that the latter was the lesser of two evils. We had traveled less than fifteen miles today, and if tomorrow were too windy, we might be stuck here for another day. Pushing onward was, really, our only option.

As we approached the northern reaches of the narrows, the rain lifted. A thick fog took its place, obscuring what we assumed to be our first glimpse of the Northern Basin. Traveling through the fog was do-able, but we were about to cross our largest bay yet. If the fog persisted and visibility remained compromised, our only option would be to trust the map and compass, hoping it led us correctly. A mistake in our bearings could cost us our lives. Furthermore, maintaining a consistent heading was complicated by a gusting wind from the north, apparently arriving earlier than predicted.

Just yards past the final structure on the western shore, we nearly wrecked when the whitecaps washed us back in the direction of the rocky embankment. At this point, the smart decision would have been to find shelter, to give in to the god of the winds, but we would not succumb to nature's test just yet. All that remained was a six-mile crossing into the wind, with a deep bay to the east and the whole of the North Basin to the north and west, hidden behind the white shield fogging our view. Neither of us could quit without completing this infamous milestone, the entrance to the uncivilized north.

If I were a betting man, I wouldn't have wagered a lot on our odds, but we eventually prevailed. Less than halfway into our blind crossing, the fog cleared and blistering wind subsided. Eventually replacing them was yet another stunning sunset amidst rolling waves. I thought back to my childhood, visiting Duluth on summer vacation. On windy days, I remembered seeing the waves come off Lake Superior, rolling like a freight train through the Lift-Bridge Canal, tossing sailboats and yachts around like dinghies. It seemed impossible for those boats to navigate such conditions, let alone a canoe. Though Lake Superior is over three times the size of Lake Winnipeg, to paddle the entirety of any lake nearing this magnitude, one must get used to paddling rollers of at least three to six feet. They seemed to occur naturally over big, open stretches of water, even when almost no noticeable wind was present. The rolling hip maneuver perfected on Big Stone Lake was a necessary expertise.

By the time we finished the crossing, night had fallen, so we stopped at the first island suitable for camping. In a lazy effort to deter black bears (who are adequate swimmers with the proper motivation), we were determined to camp away from mainland when given the opportunity. We figured it was a better deterrent than nothing. This island was nestled into a grove of similar ones, and was small and bare. Stretching no more than thirty feet across and fifty feet long, the rocky landmass had a pair of lonely trees growing at its crest, and we set up camp beside them for their feeble wind protection. Lying on my rolled out sleeping bag, I let out a sigh of relief. We survived the crossing, and three full days of Lake Winnipeg paddling were behind us. Despite our solace in successfully completing the South Basin, we knew that with each night's celebration came a new day's challenge. No longer would there be narrows or small towns for safety. The big water of Lake Winnipeg lay ahead.

Upon waking on our small island camp, we could immediately

feel a change in the weather from the previous night. Gale force winds attempted to lift our tent clear off the ground with us inside. Rolling out of my bag, I stumbled outside to get a peek of the lake's condition. The whitecaps that had nearly finished us the previous day were nothing compared to the monumental waves now staring me in the eyes. As I attempted to secure my raincoat around my shoulders, struggling against nature's fury to zip it shut, an especially large gust tore it open, nearly whipping it into the violent lake behind me. The thought of paddling out there made me sick.

"Umm, Colton, you might wanna come and check this out," I called, laughing nervously. As he crawled out of our tent, a billowing north wave crashed into our barren island, soaking us in spray. Convincing Colton that travel would be impossible was unnecessary.

It was our first weather-forced layover day since New Ulm. As this thought crossed my mind, I found it difficult to hold back a laugh. Thinking back, New Ulm seemed to be not only a completely different trip, but a different life. Four days into Lake Winnipeg, and it was already our lives. Anything before it seemed like something out of a recently read novel.

A day of rest felt wonderful. In shifts, we took turns napping while the other read and kept an eye on the lake conditions. Other than the wind, it was a beautiful day, full with clear skies and the temperature around fifty degrees Fahrenheit. Colton even made the trip's maiden cast with a fishing rod purchased in Fargo. He snagged a log on the first try and promptly resumed his sunbathing.

By 5:30 PM, the wind had slowed enough to make reasonable progress, and we jumped at the opportunity. We had no idea for how long this lake would be paddle-able, and if we hoped to maintain our strict food rations, we couldn't afford to be stranded for entire days on end.

We paddled for five hours, until we finally deemed it necessary to thaw our hands. On the sandy beach, which made up a majority of the eastern shoreline, we built a campfire out of driftwood and twigs. One of us would venture into the thick brush beyond the beach to gather more wood while the other tended to the fire, rotating to share the heat. Fueled by the breeze, the fire eventually grew so aggressive that it occasionally licked some of the hairs off our arms and brows. Too cold when we stepped away and too hot nearby, we decided the fire needed less orchestrating and more relaxation. Removing our coats, we lounged on the sand and silently stared, mesmerized by the flame.

By midnight, we set off again, hoping to make up the day's lost ground. We had paddled at night before, of course, on the Red River, and as strange as that was, this was something utterly different. A mile out from shore to avoid reefs, it was impossible to see anything but the starry sky above. Rolling up and down amongst invisible waves that we knew rose above our heads was indescribable. For direction, we used the North Star, aiming slightly to its right, ensuring that at the worst case we would run back into the eastern shore.

I sat in the bow, thinking about the hilarity of our situation, for finding the humor at times like this was our most effective coping mechanism. How could I ever articulate this properly to friends back home?

"Epic voyage," Colton muttered behind me.

CHAPTER 10

Is That Mold?

Lake Winnipeg's eastern shore along the North Basin is characterized by an endless swampy forest that backs up to sandy, unprotected beaches, not unlike our bonfire location the night of the island layover. While the sand was a welcome change in comfort from sleeping on rocks, anybody who has ever had the experience of sand camping will remark of the regret they had soon afterwards. For weeks, we were picking grains of beach out of our packs, tent, and sleeping bags.

The morning after paddling into the night came too soon. We couldn't make it all night on the water, as our natural compass was blocked by clouds sometime late, forcing us ashore. Sand sleeping comfort was brief, though, rising at 6:00 AM before the wind would inevitably reemerge.

"Is that mold?" said Colton, sitting up in the tent, yet remaining covered from shoulders to feet in his sleeping bag like a caterpillar emerging from its cocoon. He was staring at my morning slice of pizza. Hardly light enough to see the lake just outside our tent windows, and Colton had somehow spotted a growth on my breakfast.

I inspected the cheese topping closer. "I don't know. Does yours have it?"

He already had a slice in hand, but the cool morning air had chased his arms into the protected warmth of his bag. Retracting the single limb, he put his slice up to his face while I shined the flashlight at him.

"Yep," he said finally, "that's mold."

I cursed softly under my breath. We still had two full pizzas left from the town of Winnipeg, and there was little room for wasting rations.

"Maybe it's just too dark to see properly," I said. "Let's take down camp and check again with some natural light." That was it, natural light. Anything can look like mold in a flashlight's beam, I figured. It was a stretch, but I thought optimism was more constructive than panic at this juncture.

Just before pushing off the sandy beach beneath the gradually rising sun, we took a final glance at the pizza slices, now resting atop our food pack. Mold indeed. Just what we needed. Looking through our remaining slices, we saw that they were all lightly speckled in it.

"How does mold form in these temps?" I said, my optimism quickly fading. "It's thirty-three degrees out – that's colder than a fridge!"

"It's not that cold during the days, though, and it's been a week since we were in Winnipeg," said Colton.

"Oh."

"I guess we'll just have to pick it off and eat it for every meal until we run out," Colton suggested. He laughed and I shook my head. Panic had officially replaced optimism. "Hey," he added. "Penicillin comes from mold... must be good for us!"

Our morning paddle was faced with another strong north wind, depleting our already insufficient energy levels. Still in the front of the canoe, I began to feel strung out and stir-crazy. In the stern, one must constantly focus on steering, but bow paddling is a mind-numbingly boring task. Without a designated job beyond "paddle hard," thoughts became difficult to come by. Steering was far from a mental challenge, but at least it was something. I must admit, the grass was always greener on the other side; too many hours spent in the back would typically leave me itching for the roomy bow where I could let my mind drift.

By lunchtime, the wind had subsided a bit, though remained strong enough to provide a minor nuisance. After docking on the wind-shaded side of a peninsula, I leaped from the canoe into six inches of water. Desperate to feel grounded, my sore knees buckled, rolling into the moist sand upon shore. From lying on my back, I breathed deeply, taking in the sky as I felt the ground beneath me spin. Examining my hands, I noticed that my arms were unable to hold them steady. My body was shivering, though I wasn't cold. Managing to move, I plopped myself onto a boulder and stared at the ground. It was a dirt and sand combination, with rock pebbles of various sizes leading to the still water feet away. Very quickly, it was becoming evident that the lake was not only a physical challenge, but a mental one too. Was the constant bobbing in waves getting to me? Was it a lack of sleep? Something wasn't right. Colton had a blank expression on his face, though not as if in deep thought. He was in a daze. The lake was slowly taking its toll.

That afternoon, we passed the Cree First Nation at Berens River, tucked into a deep bay to the east. Our parents wanted us to stop in and restock on batteries to prevent the possibility of our SPOT Messenger dying (the light had started blinking in red instead of green), but the trip into town and back would have cost us the rest of the day, so we skipped the detour. North was the only direction in our vocabularies. Norway House, we figured, would have batteries.

As we moved further north at speeds unencumbered by the maddening curves of a river, we began gaining on our race with winter, reversing the spring thaw. It had been snowing upon our departure date in late April, and now, in early June, snow reemerged. Scattered along shore were snow banks, many stretching hundreds of feet in length. At first, we considered the possibility that polar bears had migrated to record-breaking distances south, due of course to our ungodly scent (to polar bears, we decided, the worse the smell, the more delicious the human). We eventually realized our theory was false when Colton reminded me that he put the last of his travel-sized stick of deodorant on that morning. Polar bears hate deodorant.

Instead of dashing away in fright as we initially expected, a detour to shore was in order for a break in the increasing monotony of Lake Winnipeg paddling. What began as an absentminded toss of snow towards the other (it was long-after debated who started it) turned into an all-out snowball fight. Walls and home bases were made, ammunition stores were buried, and until Colton nearly lost an eye from a rock-laden snowball, we battled like we were thirteen again. I insisted at first that Colton was faking it, preemptively calling it quits for fear of humiliating defeat. When he showed me the rock and threatened to put it through my eye to see how I liked it, I finally surrendered.

The eastern shore of Lake Winnipeg, save its entertaining snow banks, is arguably the most monotonous hundred-plus miles of lakeshore in North America. While paddling, a series of shallow bays was all we could see, each ending in the slightest of peninsulas that jutted into the lake every five to ten miles. Colton remarked that on the map it resembled the non-precise edges of an ancient flint blade. On a river, one can gauge progress by watching the constantly changing shoreline. From a mile out on Lake Winnipeg, we may as well have been paddling in place. For hours on end we sat, bobbing in the waves, staring at a hardly visible point in the distance. To our left, the west, was an endless flat of sea waves, the immensity of the lake's scale engulfing us. Eventually, I stopped looking left, for its unpredictability frightened the inland soul in me. Finally, after hours of staring at our feet, we would pass the formerly distant peninsula, and another would be visible yet again, miles further upon the horizon. Each point came and went so gradually that our progress was unnoticeable.

On the second day of the trip, way back near Belle Plaine on the Minnesota River, we had run out of material to talk about. Heck, we had been friends for so long that we likely ran out of things to talk about years before departure. Comfortable silence, after all, is the mark of true friendship. On Lake Winnipeg, for the first time in my life, I ran out of things to *think* about. Staring at my paddle dip in and out, in and out, in and out of the water, I searched the whole of my mind for any thoughts, but none came.

All the stories about wayward outcasts going insane, adrift on rubber dinghies in the middle of the ocean, made sense. Insanity was the only proper word to describe what was going on in my head, and the feeling was intoxicating. It wasn't the same intoxication as that of liquor consumption, but something close.

Finally, I voiced my feelings. After all, it had been a couple of hours since either of us had spoken. "I think I'm going insane," I said.

Colton stopped paddling. "You're kidding."

I shook my head as he turned around.

"I've stopped having thoughts," he said.

"I can't think," I said back. "I tried. I just can't."

"I've been feeling the exact same way all day!"

We noted the coincidence with brief laughter, and then we went silent once again.

On the third day of the North Basin, paddling along the shallow bays of insanity, I found myself thinking about what to think about for the better part of an afternoon. We hadn't spoken since lunch, and what had been said then was minimal. All that was left in us was the endless bobbing up and down, up and down. Staring dazedly, a thought crossed my mind... cake! I wanted food. I was hungry, yes, which was no different from the rest of the trip. But a yearning to eat sweets suddenly hit, and the thought became an obsession, a thirst unable to escape my mind. Later that night, I had a vivid dream of a friend back home smashing open a vending machine filled with pies and cakes, and gifting the stock to us as a "Welcome Home" present. The junk-food thoughts were painful, but at least they were thoughts.

Our last day of Lake Winnipeg was, as luck would have it, our most enjoyable. The night before, we accomplished something that we had been attempting for the entire lake: to watch a sunset break the surface of the water before slowly dipping into the depths below. The only two clear-sky sunsets on Lake Winnipeg had occurred within the narrows, where the western shore obscured the sun's waning moments, while clouds blocked out the sky on every other night. It was a sight for the ages, and I contemplated yielding some of my harsher sentiments towards the beast of Winnipeg.

I remember standing on a rocky point, uncharacteristic of the typical sandy beaches, staring out at the glistening water as it met the sun. It struck me how far we had come. Many people never get to experience this type of beauty, and a vast majority of those who do reach it in ease, assisted by some type of motorized technology. We made it here through nothing but our own bodies and minds. Shaking my head in awe, I smiled. Conscious thought was creeping back into my mind, proof that insanity would not be a permanent condition.

From the start of our last day, we had less than thirty miles of Lake Winnipeg left, and wonderfully calm waters to celebrate the occasion. We paddled like we were on top of the world. And we almost were. Around midday, we came upon the Spider Islands, a barren cluster of cays, scattered a mile out from shore. Noticing a set of cabins upon them, we steered into their harbor to hopefully meet a few strangers. Encountering strangers in remote cabins was always a good adventure. Almost immediately, though, it was clear that something was off. Here we were, several hundred miles into Canada, and the cabins were flying an American flag, bristling in the slight breeze. Our friendliness turned into an investigation, and we pulled ashore to take a look around.

After five minutes of peeking around the buildings, calling out to see if anybody was around, we concluded that, save the hundreds of seagulls squawking in angst at our intrusion, we were alone. Peering through the windows, we noticed magazines left open and sandwiches half-eaten. It was as though the group of people who lived here decided one day to up and leave without warning. There was something eerie about the emptiness. I had the strange feeling that we were being watched, but we could see for miles in all directions, and there wasn't another soul around.

The rest of our afternoon passed uneventfully, with the exception of us fully reenacting our favorite childhood movies. Each performance took about an hour and a half to get through, which passed the time masterfully. The lake calmed to a pane of glass as we approached Warren Landing, which marked the end of Lake Winnipeg. She had been testing us all along, ensuring we would be ready for the secluded wilderness ahead, and was now granting our passage. Failing the Lake Winnipeg test would have held dire consequences. Instead, we aced it, but it was not without a toll. One layover day and a few hazardous crossings through violent whitecaps could have resulted in flunking, but her mind games cost us our sanity. We celebrated the occasion on shore by splurging with an extra granola bar each and a few finger scoops of peanut butter. Just as we imagined Lewis and Clark celebrated after reaching the Pacific Ocean.

What used to be a small settlement with a dock for Lake Winnipeg steamboats to end their voyage was now a desolate rock-beach, with the remains of a deteriorating wooden platform resting on shore, and no town to be seen. Beyond the beach was a grown-in field with grass that grew as tall as us. We considered exploring for a few minutes, but the brush was thick enough to turn us away.

We looked back at the inland sea to our south with triumphant glee. Our quest across the big lake began in the late morning of day thirty-two, and we were finishing it near lunch of day thirty-eight. To our knowledge, six days was the fastest south to north canoe voyage across the lake since the fur traders. The last half of the lake, nearly one hundred fifty miles in length, had been so maddening that it felt like we were in a dream-state the whole time, just now stepping out of it.

Our next obstacle was the infamous Playgreen Lake. Back in Winnipeg, we had heard a variety of stories about this lake. Indeed, Sevareid himself warned of its perils in *Canoeing with the Cree*. Miniscule in comparison to Lake Winnipeg, Playgreen Lake is still vastly too large to see the opposite shore from side to side across its breadth. Size, though, was not her leading danger. Playgreen Lake is littered with so many islands, scattered in such a random order, that expert locals have been known to get lost for days or weeks at a time while boating through. Days like ours were more dangerous yet, with not a cloud in the sky or ripple in the water, causing the islands to reflect endlessly on the horizon. It was impossible to tell where the lake ended and sky began, as the islands seemed to float in midair all around us.

At some point, drifting amongst the serenity, our minds scrambled by the week on Lake Winnipeg, we lost track of our place on the map. The two of us could agree about neither where we sat at the moment, nor where to aim our canoe to move forward. After several heated minutes, growing in intensity, a plan was hatched. We would meticulously follow a compass bearing until we crossed paths with any discernible landmark. Worst-case scenario, we would miss the small river outlet to the northeast and instead end up lost in the lake for days. A cheerful thought!

We wove, seemingly aimless, in and out of islands, only ensuring that we held our compass bearing or returned to it upon reaching the far side of each island obstacle. I was sure we were heading in circles, but the compass confidently told us otherwise. Soon, though, as the sun began setting, motorboats with Cree fishermen began to pass us every few minutes, all heading in the same direction. We assumed this direction to be that of one of the most populous Cree settlements in Northern Manitoba: Norway House. If we followed their paths, we would be safe. A GPS device might have made Playgreen Lake more navigable, but a compass, map, and helping hand from the Cree, we found, would always suffice.

From the sixteen to the eighteen hundreds, the trading networks established to bring beaver fur pelts east all but ruled western Canada. In a sometimes tumultuous relationship with the Cree, the aboriginal population, traders established treaties and outposts along the most commonly used fur trade route, which stretched from the Hudson's Bay Company fort at York Factory, up the Hayes River, before finally connecting with Playgreen Lake and Lake Winnipeg at Norway House. This route was not only our intended path to Hudson Bay, but was also a point of contention among the British and French during a series of battles over rule of the region.

The fur trade was an immensely profitable business for both the natives of the land, who hunted the fur and pelt, as well as the traders and their countries. Throughout the latter half of the 17th century, the British and French fought for control over the land and the vast wealth it accompanied. During the Battle of Hudson's Bay at York Factory in 1697, the French seemingly gained the upper hand. They took control of the fort and all of the Hudson Bay watershed as a result. Within only years of French rule, however, York Factory changed hands for a final time. In the Treaty of Utrecht in 1713, which was the result of battles on European soil during the War of the Spanish Succession, the French agreed to cede York Factory to Great Britain.

Finally, in the 1763 Treaty of Paris, York Factory was unified with the rest of Canada, when it was declared to be under British rule.

Through all of the fur, money, and conflict, Norway House endured. It moved locations one time due to a massive fire, but the essence of the small Cree town remained. In the early 19th century, the settlement was created as a supply post for the popular Hayes River route to Hudson Bay. For much of the 1800s, the Hudson's Bay Company council held its annual meetings in Norway House, making decisions that would impact the exchange of millions of dollars from Canada to London.

In 2008, when Colton and I paddled ashore for a pit stop at the Hudson's Bay Store to buy groceries, little evidence of its rich history was found. Instead, we marveled at the modern amenities of SUVs in the gravel parking lot and gallon jugs of ice cream inside. Of course, we were unable to resist the temptation of chocolate ice cream, and the best deal was to buy the full gallon. Our plan to abstain from expensive snacks in the north land lasted all of five minutes. We splurged and made our dreams of sweets come true, disregarding the inconvenient reality of our freezer-less canoe.

We knew from previous travelers of the area that it would be wise to check in with the "Mounties," or the Royal Canadian Mounted Police, as they are officially called. In reality, they could hardly be considered "mounted" anymore, having ditched horses for engines some decades prior. Their camp lay at the northeast end of town on a sloping grass bank. It was a pretty location and difficult to miss, paddling through the settlement. While the Mounties were marginally interested in our future travels towards Hudson Bay, they actually seemed to be more puzzled by a caller who had been frequenting their phone line. Nick Coleman, from the Minneapolis *Star Tribune*, had called several times in case we stopped in, urging us to call him back.

Our conversation with Nick was lengthy, so while one talked on the phone, the other chatted with the Mounties and wandered around the grounds. We learned that the economy of Norway House is largely dependent on the season. In the summer months, when fishing and trapping is abundant, the town seems like a quaint tourist destination. In the winter, things are more bleak, with unemployment rates as high as 60% to 70%, and alcoholism growing rampant. Norway House, a "dry" community that outlaws alcohol, faces the challenge of enforcing prohibition in a land where hiding spots and hunting shacks are abundant. In fact, we were told that the abandoned cabins from our last day on Lake Winnipeg were likely owned by bootleggers, used as a staging point for their smuggling operations.

After forty-five minutes on the phone, Mr. Coleman insisted that we pose for a picture with the Mounties. Outside by one of their police cars, we smiled for a picture that would be posted on the newspaper's front page the following day. The picture turned out to more resemble a mug shot, as our smiles came across instead like grimaces. The long days on the water and our temporary bout with insanity had scarred our faces with perpetual boredom. We were certain that friends and distant relatives would be calling our parents upon seeing the headline, wondering how we managed to get arrested in the Canadian bush.

We bid farewell to our temporary hosts and pushed off onto the Nelson River. Leaving Norway House, we wouldn't see civilization again until we reached Oxford House, another Cree settlement several hundred miles ahead. The Nelson eventually flows all the way from Playgreen Lake to Hudson Bay and was, originally, our planned route. It, as we initially thought, contained fewer rapids and was a more direct path. Since the 1950s, however, Manitoba Hydro has constructed a series of hydroelectric dams on the river, which now power nearly all of Manitoba.

As with any man-made construction in once pristine waters, imminent controversy surrounded the projects. Their impact on the local Cree communities and the wildlife on which they depend has been largely negative. Lake Winnipeg is the largest in a series of massive reservoirs created by the dams, terracing the majority of the Nelson River's descent to Hudson Bay. In so doing, they render what was once a natural mix of lakes and rivers, into unending flat-water, changing the environment and the inhabitants suited to it irreparably. Of course, the vast majority of Manitoba residents benefit from the relatively clean power supply and live far-removed from the direct natural consequences, causing most of the controversy to fizzle quietly.

While researching route options in the time leading up to our departure, we learned of the dams and were warned of their dangers. They were unlike those of the Minnesota and Red rivers, which paled in comparison. Horror stories told of unsuspecting travelers getting too close, becoming entrapped into the wicked current above the dams, and being funneled into their powerful depths. Beyond the dangers, we were most turned away from the Nelson River route by the altered scenery and wildlife. We instead settled on the Hayes River, which was the more renowned, and preserved, fur trade route.

Twenty-five miles after Norway House, the Nelson River continues northward, and a tiny channel from the east flows in. This channel, called the Echimamish River, translates in Cree to "Water that runs in two directions." Despite its implausibility, the word in town was that this actually was the case. Halfway through this nearly forty-mile creek is a shallow marsh, which sits squarely on the divide between the Nelson and Hayes watersheds. Legend has it that the water from there flows downward on both sides. Eventually, just after the famous Painted Stone Portage, the Echimamish merges with the northeast flowing Hayes River, which would carry us the remaining four hundred miles to Hudson Bay.

"Carry us" may be misleading, as the challenges between Norway House and Hudson Bay would be many. First and foremost, when compared to the free flowing rapids of the Hayes River, the once-intimidating low-head dams on the Red River were mere dribbles. With limited true whitewater experience, running the prevalent stretches of rapids that define the Hayes would be a "learn-as-we-go" type of process. Though there were several dozens of rapids between here and the bay, one particular part, just after Knee Lake (the second of two major lakes left on our route), we dubbed the "rapids section." Forty miles of near-constant whitewater, waterfalls, and boulders, all through a maze of islands and back channels, would end with White Mud Falls, the last rapids before the Bay.

After White Mud, the Hayes grows in width and power, multiplying by each factor as it takes on the Fox and God's rivers. The final one hundred twenty miles of our voyage would indeed be rapid-less, but the width of the river valley, coupled with its environment transitioning from the forested Boreal Shield ecosystem into the tundra-like Hudson Plains, often makes for inhospitable conditions. It is said that only a dozen groups attempt to paddle the Hayes River in its entirety each year, and many never make it to this final stretch. Typically, these groups began their journeys at Norway House, and with far less skin in the game, Colton and I assumed that they bowed out under lesser circumstances than we would. After all, we had made it this far. Hudson Bay or bust.

From Norway House to York Factory, much of the land remains unchanged from the days of French and British fur trade. The locals continue to hunt, trap, and fish to support their ways of life, and beyond the reaches of the two Cree nations, humans are few and far between. We were guests in a home that, at best, tolerated us.

Back outside of Norway House, prior to reaching the Echimamish River, we passed an island, slightly smaller than the size of a football field, covered in mounds of trash. This was their dump. The smell reminded me of an overcrowded beach on a hot summer day. I wondered how a people who were so reliant on the local ecosystem could allow such a spectacle, but decided that one ruined island was better than tarnishing an entire forest. They were concentrating the pollution. It occurred to me that, despite the similar look and feel of Norway House to a northern Minnesota town, it was a Cree reserve, and we were far removed from the laws and regulations of our home country.

That night, camping on an island in the center of Sea River Falls, eighteen river-miles past Norway House, we realized that back home, today was the last day of school. We felt so separated from them, both literally and figuratively. They were likely celebrating their "freedom" from strenuous time spent learning in a warm and dry classroom with friends. Perhaps, if the urge so struck, they would indulge in a burger at the local diner. Meanwhile, we were celebrating the start of our final leg of the trip: a wilderness jump of over four hundred miles through some of the most secluded wilderness in North America. And we were celebrating in our two-person tent over a tub of melted chocolate ice cream.

Typical mornings throughout the voyage, whether it was late April or early June, started cold. The morning after Norway House was considerably warmer than most, registering a whopping forty-nine degrees Fahrenheit. A misty haze covered the Nelson River valley, though, contrasting with the sunny skies that we had enjoyed the previous two days.

Just around the river bend from our camp, we saw evidence on shore of the ferry that connects the roads of Norway House to the rest of Canada, leading eventually to a highway to the north. The road, technically a "winter-road," is manageable to drive in the summer months, but only for the most rugged off-road vehicles.

Onward we paddled through the haze, watching for the Echimamish River trickling in from the east. We knew from our maps that there would be a tall rock wall at the confluence, but that due to its size, the river itself could be easy to miss. To complicate matters, the Nelson River split into a maze of channels, all appearing to be equal in size. Traveling north and knowing that we would eventually have to split off to the east, we kept to the right, hoping that it would lead us correctly.

Finally, there it was: a massive cliff overhanging the river straight ahead. Just to the right was a small stream hidden under the shade of poplar trees and pines.

"What is that white thing on the tree there?" Colton wondered aloud.

I looked between the cliff and the mouth of the Echimamish and noticed a white sign with black print mounted to a tree.

"It's a sign. What's it say?"

Floating closer, we discovered that there were actually two signs stacked upon each other. The top one said "Route," with an arrow pointing to the stream on our right. The other, in all capital letters, read "ECHIMAMISH RIVER."

We could hardly contain our laughter. Here we were, imagining ourselves as true explorers at the frontier of civilization.

"Do you suppose there will be signs like this the whole way?" I asked.

"I hope not," said Colton. "Either way, let's not tell anybody about it." We never did see signs like these again.

The band of Cree who inhabit the Hudson Bay watershed are considered to be "Swampy Cree." I finally understood why, as the Echimamish River meandered its way through low-lying marsh for the majority of its course. Our initial worry of paddling upstream again, anticipating flashbacks of the Minnesota River, turned out to be for folly. The stiffness of the current mimicked the Red River.

During our lunch break on a pretty bit of high ground, beneath a sprawling willow tree, we heard the misplaced sound of a motor in the distance.

"Wufs vat?" I said through a mouthful of rice. I was crouched down like a baseball catcher over my plate, about ten feet away from the river.

Colton, sitting with his back to a tree facing the water, rolled out to the bank and scanned the vicinity. "I don't see anything," he said.

The sound grew louder, and soon we found, with excitement, that a boat was approaching. Other humans – always a treat! As quickly as it came, the boat zoomed by, giving us only enough time to recognize that there were two passengers aboard. Likely having just barely seen us as they passed, the boat sharply turned about and then coasted ashore at our feet.

It was a basic aluminum fishing boat with a tiller-operated motor hanging off of the back. The man operating the boat was a bulky elderly gentleman, who wore a natural look of ease across his face. In front was a more slender man, appearing to be in his thirties or forties. Both were Cree. As they pulled ashore, none of us spoke. I believe they were as surprised to see us as we were them. Moving beyond the awkward silence, I took the initiative and introduced us both.

"We're heading up to Hudson Bay," I said, following with our names.

The older man in the back looked at our canoe. I assumed that he was judging it in some way.

"From Minneapolis," he said, noticing the stickers on the side of our boat. "In the States?"

We nodded. "We left in April." I waited for a skeptical response.

The man smiled briefly in approval. "My name's David; this is Erik. Not sure why you boys would want to do what you're doing, but alright."

Colton began to defend our reasoning, which I suspected mattered little to these men, but before he could muster a word, David continued.

"Doing any fishing?"

"Not much," I said. "We tried back on Lake Winnipeg but just caught snags."

"Shame!" said David. "These are some of the best waters in the world."

As it turned out, our new friends were trappers and fishermen from Norway House, out for a two-day job. Erik appeared jittery, scratching aimlessly at the side of their boat while we spoke. Catching his young partner's cue that they were in a hurry, David pushed back off into the stream before long. It was a short interaction, but we passed them again about an hour later anchored in the middle of the river, throwing nets out of their boat. For commercial fishermen in Cree villages like Norway House, netting was a far more productive approach than rod and reel.

Not long after lunch, rain began to pour. It dripped down the hoods to our raincoats and caught in our increasingly full, albeit patchy, facial hair. The temperature dropped dramatically, approaching freezing, and I worried my bearded cheeks would harden to icicles. We found ourselves exposed to another strong headwind and driving rain, as the open marshland that the Echimamish passed through did little to break up weather.

By early evening, the weather had exhausted our energy, and we came to a spot where a beaver dam blocked the width of the river ahead. We took this to be the reason behind the minimal water flow. In the same sentence that we thanked the critters for making our upstream paddle possible, we cussed at them for their obstacles. A part of me felt as if they were punishing us for our European ancestors and their relentless hunt for the pelts of the beaver's great-great-great-grandparents.

Colton was in the bow, so he made the first attempt to pull our canoe over the dam alone. He climbed out, stepping onto the stick-bridge. Upon receiving his weight, the dam dumped Colton into the stream, his foot sinking in a rush of water. This wouldn't be as easy as we hoped. Our next attempt involved pulling up to the dam sideways, and both of us simultaneously stepping out and pulling upwards.

"Argh!"

Nearly tipping the canoe in the process, we jumped back in and sat, staring at the heap of branches blocking our way. On the Minnesota River, we had crossed beaver dams and logjams that dwarfed our current foe, but the wind had picked up and rain was now blowing into our faces, piercing our skin and exposed eyes. I put my head in my hands and searched my mind for not just a solution, but also perseverance.

"Curse all the beavers!" I yelled into the faded sky.

"I don't know, man," said Colton. "Should we just call it a night and tackle the dam tomorrow? Hopefully, it'll be nicer out and we can dress our feet for lining."

Colton always had the best ideas.

CHAPTER 11

Adventure We Would Face

At 5:30 AM, our alarm echoed off of the tent walls. It was light out, and I could hear the rain continue its relentless pounding of the forest floor. Our tent sat in a clearing upon a sloped rock, exposed to the sky, so I knew that the water droplets on our roof were not the result of trees dripping old rain from above. I hit the alarm's snooze bar and closed my eyes for another moment, dreading for when I would have to go "out there" again.

The next time my eyes opened, it was 8:00 AM, and Colton was still asleep beside me. Inside our tent, the temperature remained in the high thirties, and rain had yet to cease. The tent floor had soaked through overnight, and water was seeping into our sleeping bags. I knew that the smartest thing to do would be to wake Colton and be on our way, but closing my eyes one more time seemed far more enjoyable.

At 9:45 AM, Colton and I awoke simultaneously and agreed to be on our way. It had been a morning of weakness for us both, admitting to each other that we knew we were being lazy but simply didn't care. The weather had hardly improved since our alarm first rang, but our bodies were now soaked through, and I wanted nothing more than to get out of the tent. It's amazing how being wet and cold can motivate a person.

"Let's just go," said Colton firmly as we packed our last bag into the canoe. The tent was still wet and stuffing it into its pack would only aggravate that matter, but there were no other options. "The tent is going to be wet for days now. Same with our sleeping bags. Let's just finish this damn trip and get to a warm bed."

A warm bed. That was all I needed to hear. "Yeah, let's go."

Without having breakfast, we left, moving with a purpose. We conquered in minutes the very beaver dam that ended our day the night previous. Though the beaver dams increased in frequency, so did our pace. It was raining, but that merely lessened our concern with getting our feet wet. Each subsequent dam became more efficient to hop over until they would hold us up for no more than ten to twenty seconds.

Near midday, we noticed a tiny cabin hidden within the dark forest, smoke rising out of its chimney. We recognized the boat on shore to be David and Erik's. Figuring that they had passed us late last night or early this morning while we were still in our tent, we invited ourselves to knock on the door to join them during our lunch break.

The smell of fresh bacon met our nostrils as we walked in, and the sound of its grease popping punctured the silence. A one-room cabin, it was lit by a single lantern in the center of a wooden table, opposite the stove. Next to the back wall were two well-worn cots. It wasn't much, but I considered how wonderful of a sleep it would have been had we made it this far last night. To the left of the entrance sat David, stoking the fire in a pot-bellied stove. They were excited to see Colton and me, and invited us in to share their meal.

"Is this your cabin?" I asked.

"No," said David. "It's nobody's. Just for trappers or weather-stranded travelers."

We certainly qualified as the latter, so the thought of spending the day here tugged at my heartstrings. Our late morning had already wasted enough time, though, and the last few hours had been some of our strongest paddling in weeks. We compromised by taking our Cree friends up on their offer of a warm lunch.

David, we found out, was highly regarded back in Norway House and had a particular talent for storytelling. Hunting and trapping on the Echimamish seemed to be his true passion, but netting fish paid the bills. Erik, David's son-in-law, spoke no more than a word or two the whole time. He sat at the table next to us, observing silently and laughing softly at the appropriate moments, all the while puffing on a series of hand-rolled cigarettes.

The bacon was delicious, but our conversation amidst the smoke-filled room was a dream come true. In 1930, Sevareid and Port traveled for several days with Cree paddlers, learning their customs and way of life. We didn't grow as close to our Cree friends as they had, but the experience was something I could have never imagined. Before departing, David gave us his contact information on a business card and offered to take us out moose hunting if we were ever in the area again. The gesture was unbelievable, though I doubted that Sevareid and Port's Cree companions carried business cards.

Over the afternoon, our two parties leap-frogged several times, passing each other every few hours. One such leapfrog was at the famous Painted Stone Portage, where the Echimamish slid down a twenty-foot rock slope that we had incorrectly assumed signified the start of the Hayes River. We would not begin the Hayes for another ten miles, but we were quite unaware of that fact, so we celebrated this as the unofficial beginning of our descent to Hudson Bay. This little trickle of water, we knew, would carry us for the next four hundred miles.

The name of the portage, which was actually a sacred point of worship for some of the more traditional Cree, comes from the ancient pictographs along a rock wall that bordered us on our right. Lying along the stone slab, connecting the two pools, was a portage ladder made out of neatly carved tree trunks. The giant ladder-like structure was made of two long logs, stretched parallel to each other down the length of the slight hill, with ten shorter logs on their top, bridging the gap perpendicularly. I had used a similar contraption at my family cabin growing up while landing our pontoon boat, so its purpose was fairly clear.

Before we had a chance to test the portage ladder, David and Erik rolled up in their boat from behind. Wordlessly, we moved our outfit out of their way as they passed us, equally silent. We were beyond small talk, so a simple nod sufficed as a respectful interaction. It was a real treat to watch them at work. Effortlessly, they got out of their boat and stood on each side, lifting it onto the ladder, then guiding the vessel down the hill to the water at the bottom. The moment their boat was floating, they jumped back in, dropped and started the motor, then whisked away. If only landing our pontoon at the cabin had worked that well! My parents would have admired their portaging abilities as an act of art.

Surely Colton and I could have carried our canoe down the hill, just as we had on the low-head dams of the Red River. After watching the Cree masters at work, though, the portage ladder looked far too enjoyable to pass up.

Soon, we passed the point where the Echimamish merged with the Hayes, along with our final intersection with David and Erik. They would remain on the Echimamish for the day and then head back to Norway House at nightfall. As nice as that sounded, moving forward had become our obsession.

That night, we camped on the wind-protected side of a peninsula that stretched out to the middle of Robinson Lake. At the eastern end of the lake, reserved for the following morning, was a mile-long portage around Robinson Falls. Knowing that we didn't have the energy for such a portage to conclude our day, we finished early and enjoyed the freshly cloudless sky by exploring the terrain around our camp.

The peninsula was densely wooded and largely comprised of a steep hill. While hiking to the other side, hoping to catch a glimpse of our morning's paddle, we called out loudly to each other in an effort to warn bears of our movement. The calls began mild-mannered but eventually turned into well-meaning insults. It was the perfect excuse to let off some steam, as an unspoken agreement provided us immunity from anything said while scaring away bears. We figured, if nothing else, the bears would be frightened by our downright cruelty toward one another.

Each morning seemed colder than the last, though the daylight was growing longer as we moved further north, and the Earth's orbit gradually approached its summer solstice. After a late start the previous day, and realizing that continuing to wake up when it was already light out wasted valuable time, we resolved to move up our wake-up call to 4:30. It would still be dark, but by the time we were packed up and on the water, the sun would be over the horizon, illuminating the world and warming its landscape. Plus, starting early would provide us the freedom to finish early guilt-free if the weather or our muscles so dictated.

As we rounded the bend of our camp's peninsula, out into the open lake, we were exposed to the prevailing winds from the east. For ten minutes, we were blown backward, losing ground on our destination. Instead of calming down as we had hoped, the wind had exceeded its force from the day before. Frustration with the weather was mounting exponentially as the days progressed.

Sitting in the bow, windblown tears of anger ran secretly down my face. I was frustrated with every part of my life. I could no longer remember what it was like to wake up warm, dry, and satisfied with my night's sleep. While the initial wave of anger dissipated quickly, a part of it lingered for the remainder of the trip. Sevareid and Port came to blows during the most trying times of the north country. They were much nearer the bay than us when it happened, but I knew that the Canadian wilderness would eventually take its toll. The question wasn't *if* it would test our team; it was when and how much? A fistfight nearly killed Sevareid and Port and permanently scarred their friendship. I hoped desperately that we would conquer the north before it conquered us.

The Hayes River was, for the next few hundred miles, a series of lakes connected by rivers and rapids. While the continuous change in scenery was welcome, attempting to locate the river's outlet from each lake became a perpetual challenge. At the northeast end of Robinson Lake, we searched for fifteen minutes, following the shoreline back and forth, before finally locating Robinson Portage through a thicket of overgrown brush.

At the end of the portage, where we were supposed to set our canoe back in the water and launch out, we were greeted with mud that was comparable to that of the Red River. My shoulders were groaning under the pressure of two packs, so I opted to make the first attempt to navigate the muck. Being a lifelong klutz, something was bound to go wrong. Indeed, just two steps in, I fell. From the bottom, I was pulled by the muck, from the top, pinned by my own gear. Thank goodness Colton was able to take a break from his merciless laughter long enough to come to my aid. Had he rolled around on the ground any longer, he might have gotten stuck himself.

Floating slowly down a lazy bit of the Hayes during a granola break, Colton reached for that section's page of the book, *Wilderness Rivers of Manitoba*, by Hap Wilson, which we had torn from our copy back home. These pages would be our saving grace along the Hayes River, we hoped. Our topographical Manitoba maps, which were useful on Lake Winnipeg, continued to cover the land all of the way to Hudson Bay, but they were far too zoomed out to be of any help in the rapids-heavy segments. Hap Wilson's book, on the other hand, filled this void nicely, providing the locations and detailed diagrams of each set of whitewater along our route. Now, as we approached the first set of such difficult sections, a brief lapse in focus cost us greatly.

Being the stern-man also meant being the navigator, so Colton, sitting in the back, began carefully planning our first few miles of major rapids. We had studied our route for months, years even. We could tell you, off-hand, the order of the lakes, and all of the major landmarks between them. But that was no replacement for having a map of our surroundings spread-out before us. Habitually, we would white-knuckle each map in the rain and wind, knowing that they were critical to our success. Despite that, Colton inexplicably set this one loosely on top of our rig, and before even being able to look away, it was gone, whipped into the distance by the wind. We sat stunned, knowing we would have to judge the upcoming rapids by sight alone.

Around the next bend, we saw the adrenaline pumping view of the river ahead forming a horizontal line and then disappearing from view. Beyond the line, spouts of water splashed upward into view like miniature geysers.

We pulled ashore fifty yards upstream and climbed a shrubby cliff to catch a scout-able view. The rapids were treacherous. Halfway down was a ninety-degree turn to the left with a five-foot standing wave. It stood precisely at the apex of the curve, and this alone was enough for me to say no, without even factoring the multiple ledges of two to three feet spread throughout. I opted for portaging. Colton however, always the risk taker, wanted some adventure, or perhaps a chance to re-prove his river-worthiness. Either way, as was our means of settling every dispute, we flipped a coin, or in this case a cracker, to decide. Colton won.

We took five minutes to tie down our gear. All the while, my stomach churned at the relentless sound of water crashing on rock. If the goal was adventure, adventure we would have. I don't blame Colton for wanting to run the rapids – the thrill was actually enticing in a way.

It was apparent immediately upon entering the falls that we had screwed up. In fact, it was apparent several feet before. Running rapids is a team effort. The dependence a bowman has on his partner is obvious, but I had a critical role as well. It goes against human nature, but aside from spotting obstructions and calling directions, the most important task for the person in the front is to simply paddle as hard as they can. If the canoe has less speed than the water it's riding on, your path is fully at the mercy of where the current chooses to take you. In order to actually steer the craft, it's vital to move fast. The science behind the theory makes sense, but to nearly every unseasoned rapid runner, all theory goes out the window as you're crashing through waves and spray, pointed directly at a half-submerged boulder. Instead, every instinct in your body says one thing: SLOW DOWN. It's the bowman's job to fight this instinct.

In milliseconds, we cruised down the initial drop and even executed the proper turn at the ninety-degree bend. It was the standing wave, though, that proved to be too much, hitting our broadside and filling the canoe with water. We reeled, attempting to avoid a rollover, and the canoe turned about, facing backwards downstream.

As we had planned in advance for a situation like this, we turned our bodies around frantically and traded the duties of steering and paddling. It was surprising that we each had the wherewithal to remember this maneuver, as the rest of my mind was blank. Everything was happening so fast, yet time stood still. Each droplet of water that sprayed in our faces appeared to move in slow motion, their contours clear as day. The adrenaline had kicked in, and my mind was razor-focused.

In the chaos of turning around, we slid sideways over a three-foot ledge, and time sped up again. We bobbed further down the foaming water before getting caught again, this time on an exposed boulder. Colton stuck his leg out into the current to keep us from tipping, and we made brief eye contact. Our faces said it all: panic. For what felt like a minute we sat, wedged between the unyielding torrent and rock, water pouring into our canoe faster than we could comprehend. The makeshift spray skirt was helping, but dozens of gallons of water per second were testing the Velcro adhesive that held the skirt to the gunnels. Any longer and the weight would tear the spray skirt clear off, allowing the river free rein to pull our entire outfit under.

This was it. This was how our trip would end. It was impossible to see how we would get out of this with an intact canoe and enough of our gear to continue on, let alone our lives. If one of us were to fall out, our unprotected heads would be vulnerable to any rock below the surface. We had come all this way, and this would be our end.

Fate, though, had a different plan, and a fortunate surge in the current twisted us around, sliding us off the rock and backwards over another ledge. That was it; the section of whitewater had ended. We coasted out of the last bits of fastwater breathlessly. Neither of us spoke for minutes, kneeling on the floor of the canoe in water up to our waists. The gunnels were only inches from submersion.

We found ourselves in a small lagoon, with a sloped rock outcrop falling into the water at the closest shore. Slowly but surely, we made our way to it. Getting out would have been difficult if we cared about getting wet, but our soaked lower bodies were beyond concern as we stepped into the shallow water to pull up the canoe.

Colton laughed anxiously. "That was fun!"

For a few hours there, we enjoyed a rare sunny and windless moment, sheltered by our pond-like backwater. It was a lucky coincidence that one of our few sunny days on the Hayes River came at a time when it was necessary to dry out our luggage and rest our nerves.

This break also happened to coincide with the lunch hour, so with every bit of our equipment strewn about, lying in the sun upon that rock, we feasted. We fried the pizza that remained salvageable, and then regrettably tossed the rest. It would hurt our rations immensely, but after a week of eating moldy pizza, we had enough. When we found our hunger yet unquenched, a lonely holdover gift from a well-wisher along the Minnesota River appeared amidst our ruins: a can of Spam, delicious, salty, fatty, and waiting to be devoured. When one is hungry enough, anything can be a feast. That day on the rock, eating our Spam and pizza lunch, we were kings.

CHAPTER 12

A Tale of Bear Spray

Hells Gate Gorge: famous for its natural beauty and infamous for its treacherous, un-portage-able, multi-mile stretch of rapids with sheer rock walls on either side. Only miles from the scene of our latest whitewater fiasco, we were forced to jump right back into it. We joked that now our lack of maps didn't matter, for if there were any unexpected falls, we wouldn't be able to leave the deep-cut channel anyhow. Perhaps it was a blessing in disguise, not allowing us the chance to overthink ourselves and grow timid in rapids. After all, the best way to learn is failure.

We learned from our practice voyages that success in rapids required a multitude of strategies. There was the standard portage, as I often leaned towards. For the more adventurous souls, like Colton, there was the obvious all-liquid descent. There was also a third choice, however, something of an in-between: lining. Just as we did during fast stretches on the Minnesota River, like in downtown Mankato and Granite Falls, we would get out and pull the canoe, in this case safely down un-runnable rapids. In Hells Gate, and more generally, in fact, all three methods were used. The gorge was a frantic episode, but our ability to find calm back-eddies in the midst of fastwater played a crucial role in evaluating strategy on the fly. Climbing in and out of the canoe was burdensome, but necessary.

At the end of Opiminegoka Lake, we came across another abandoned cabin, not unlike those claimed by bootleggers on the Lake Winnipeg archipelago. This time, we decided against investigating due to time constraints. The sun was going down and we wanted to reach our goal for the day. We spent the night in the middle of Windy Lake on the smallest island we had camped on yet. No larger than twenty by twenty feet, the tiny rock felt like little more than a reef in the open sea. It was also a perfect location for seagulls to dispose of their waste. Needless to say, we awoke to a polka-dotted tent.

From the outlet of Windy Lake into the Hayes River, we once again were forced to jump back into whitewater. At one point, in an attempt to cut corners, we squeezed our little green canoe between a tiny crevice separating shore and a tall stone cleaved from it. Throughout the morning, we continued to run into shallow stretches, forcing us to line frequently. Upon reaching one portage that crossed over a narrow strip of land, we encountered a ladder similar to the one at the Painted Stone Portage. The presence of this level of "technology" told us that we were nearing a human settlement.

The settlement was Oxford House, a Cree village that lies at the east end of Oxford Lake, far from the southwest corner in which the Hayes River enters. It is a lake that pales in comparison to Lake Winnipeg, yet remains massive in its own right. From what we had heard about Oxford House, it was a smaller, rougher version of Norway House. In Hap Wilson's book, he mentions stories of white paddlers visiting, and Cree children throwing rocks at them, urging the guests not to linger. Regardless of the truth behind this tale, we decided that we would play it safe and camp, later that night, at least a few miles short of the village.

For the first several miles of Oxford Lake, we struggled, bucking the wind along the southwestern shore. Relentless wind from the east was becoming our cruel reality. A group of islands lined the middle of the lake, but they did little to block the insistent gusts from reaching us. After two hours of painstaking struggle, making less than a mile of progress, we decided that a break was needed. Once again, we used the time to make lunch and air out the wet components of our perpetually soaked equipment. In the woods, secluded from the obnoxious wind, the weather was actually quite nice. It was hard to believe that some twenty feet away, white caps tumbled across the gigantic lake, taunting us with their power.

For three hours, we enjoyed our sunny enclosure, taking turns napping, reading, and standing guard for bears. The book we had been reading since Wahpeton was a story about a young boy on an adventure with his dragon and mentor. It wasn't my usual cup of tea, but with the exception of the magical beast, it felt as though we were reading about our own adventure. We were entertained, at least, by drawing parallels between the two.

Eventually, it was once again time to go. Our destination routed us diagonally across the lake to the northeast corner, and crossing the main bay would be hazardous in the current due-east winds. Colton suggested we break conventional wave-paddling wisdom and paddle north, broadsiding the wind through a wide strait before heading east, using the lee-side of islands to leapfrog our way up the lake. It meant a significant detour, but also a break from our nemesis. Expert and novice paddlers alike would call our route suicide, insisting that the smartest and safest way to deal with a strong headwind is to quarter it at a forty-five degree angle. We, on the other hand, found quartering to be a lose-lose proposition, as it caused the stern to fishtail with each wave, which in turn forced us to regularly correct our direction.

Weaving in and out of island-protected waters, this slow-moving process eventually worked. We spent the remainder of our day zigzagging across Oxford Lake, humming tunes to ourselves and each other, and finding solace in the wind-free moments.

One location lent itself to another break, when we gravitated towards some attractive high ground on what appeared to be a massive island. A bit of fun was in order, and so with our bear spray in hand, we took a hike. As kids in the Boundary Waters, we would spend our days hiking as far as the game trails off our campsites ventured, and then would forge our own path further with hatchets and machetes. We would carry the wood remains all the way back to camp to be used in the fire pit when our fathers returned from a day of fishing, always with a stringer full of fresh walleye to satisfy our hard-earned appetites. It was a mutually sustaining way of life, and it fit our pleasures splendidly. Our dads lived for fishing. Colton and I lived for exploring. Now exploring this remote island on Oxford

Lake, we used the same hatchet to make our way around the pathless venture, though unfortunately, the debris was never used for firewood.

At the highest point we cared to travel sat a treeless clearing, the rocky floor unwilling to allow roots to make a home within its domain. Here we stopped and looked to the south, scanning miles upon miles of forested beauty. Scattered about were lakes and rivers, each with their own sets of rapids. If Fairmount, North Dakota was a farmer's God's Country, this was ours.

A gust of wind blew through the open clearing and ruffled my greasy hair. It had been weeks since our last shower, the lakes and rivers too cold to even contemplate swimming. We hardly cared, though; after all, who did we have to impress? I had taken my wool hat off for the hike, but I was reminded by the wintry breeze that freezing temperatures would be on their way as night drew nearer. With that in mind, we settled back down to the water's edge to continue onward. Adventures on land were fun, but so too was the adventure ahead.

During the days of fur trading, Oxford House started as a wayside rest and eventually became a permanently settled community when the United Church of Canada sent Protestant ministers and families to the post. Unlike Norway House, there are no outside roads connected to the village, even by ferry, so supplies can only make their way to the store's shelves through air travel. This economic isolation resulted in an additional layer of seclusion from the outside world, evident in the wilder feel the town generally had. Primitive and proudly uncivilized was Oxford House's mark of distinction.

Our morning in town, the second day on Oxford Lake, turned out to be a disorganized jumble of miniature escapades. Wary of large open spaces where airborne rocks from disgruntled children could easily reach us, we pulled ashore before town and hiked up a densely wooded hill. At the top, we found ourselves in a desolate wasteland. A gravel road stretched to our left and right, parallel to the shoreline, and ahead was a parking lot with tin-sided buildings on each side. There was one pick-up truck in the lot, and on the other side was another gravel road heading to the left and right. Either due to the scrubby vegetation of the land or the sparse buildings, it felt like a town on the wild western frontier. I half expected to hear the sound of a creaky swinging door from a nearby saloon, straight from a John Wayne film. After hiking down the dirt road for ten minutes without encountering another soul, we determined that this must not be the part of town that we were looking for and promptly made our way back to the canoe.

Around the next peninsula was a gently sloped field facing the lake and a prominent tin building resting on its top. Finally, what we were looking for; it was a "Northern Store," a grocery mainstay in Cree communities. Approaching the front door, we saw, nailed up, a black and red sign that read "CLOSED."

"You suppose we should knock?" asked Colton. It must have been rhetorical, because he gave the door a sharp rap just as he asked.

An older Cree man came to the door, looking ruffled. "Who are you?" Outsiders were clearly rare.

We gave him our standard spiel.

"We don't open until 9:00," he said, apparently choosing not to acknowledge our trip or circumstances.

I looked at the watch on my wrist. It was typically wrapped around the thwart in front of the stern seat, but I liked to bring it with when we left our outfit. We had paddled for several hours already this morning, and the sun was now high enough in the sky to warm the day substantially. If I had guessed, I would have assumed it was just past lunchtime, but the watch disagreed, reading 8:30 AM. The abandoned nature of the town now made sense.

"Oh," I said sheepishly. "We'll come back later."

Adjacent to the Northern Store was another gravel road. It led up a hill along shore back towards where we had first pulled over, so I assumed it was the very same one. We scanned the area for a moment, contemplating our next move.

"Hey! Are you Colton and Sean?"

From across the road, beneath the awning of a meticulously wood-sided home, a man motioned to us. Marvin, we learned, had heard about us in Norway House. He worked with Manitoba Conservation and let us fill up our water jugs inside. We chatted for some time, and before departing, he directed us to the RCMP station a half mile up the road.

To save time, we split up, and while I checked in with the Mounties, Colton stopped back at the Northern Store to fill up on supplies. Our frequent layovers since Norway House and the moldy pizza had diminished our rations, so a re-supply was more critical than we had anticipated.

It was one of only a handful of times throughout the trip that Colton and I split up. I hummed to myself while walking up the sandy road to the police station. The day was now warm enough that my fleece sweatpants and sweatshirt were beginning to make me sweat. My boots were far from ideal on the soft ground, so every few steps, I rolled my ankles over clumsily. Looking back toward the Northern Store, I saw that Colton had already disappeared inside, and I felt alone. It was a welcome feeling at first, relieving, actually. After a minute or two, though, I began to feel out of place. Spending every second with a person for weeks on end apparently has its effects.

At the Mountie station, tucked in the woods beyond the main road, I checked the weather and told the two officers on duty of our plans and intended schedule. We had been informed that it was important to have these conversations with local officials in case for some reason we were to go missing.

"Not to worry, though," I said after providing our eventual destination. "We have a SPOT messenger that'll tell our parents exactly where we are in case of an emergency. There's even an emergency button on it."

One officer looked at the other with an amused smile. In the thickest of accents, he proceeded to burn our insurance policy. "Sorry to inform you, eh, but out on the last couple hundred kilometers of the Hayes, there's no emergency evacuation coming. If you're stuck, you better hope you can last a few days for a boat from Shamattawa to come save you."

"What about the rapids section?"

"Doubtful as well," said the officer. "I suppose I should have said the last *three* hundred kilometers. Once you pass Swampy Lake, just after Knee Lake, you're on your own. We've had some other travelers pass through that area, but nobody I know has ever done it. That's no-man's land. No safe landing for choppers, and floatplanes are usually too booked to set off on a rescue mission at the drop of a hat. Won't land in inclement weather either, which it looks like you boys will have."

"Okay. . ." I trailed off. I wasn't sure exactly why I was even checking in if the Mounties couldn't do anything for us during the most dangerous portion of the trip. "Well, you know where we're headed, then. We're hoping to make Swampy Lake in two days."

I stayed for a few minutes to watch the weather forecast scroll across a small television in the main room of the station. Chatting more personally with the Mounties, I realized that while they were genuinely kind, they were trained to be wary of over-confident tourists traveling through their territory. Too often, inexperienced explorers attempt to venture into the wilderness, their foolhardiness creating an annoying liability for the local officers.

According to the Canadian weather service, we would have one more day after today of quality travel conditions, but things looked dismal beyond that. Possible snow, temperatures hovering around freezing, and wind filled the forecast. I hoped that it would be better a couple hundred miles to the north, our eventual route, but seriously doubted it.

"Just make sure you don't camp or spend too much time on shore closer than ninety or a hundred kilometers from the bay." I searched my brain for the conversion rate... fifty or sixty miles, I figured. "That's polar bear country. It's been a late winter, so there's a good chance they're still out on the bay-ice, but food is scarce up there and polar bears have a keen sense of smell. They'll catch your scent from any closer than that." We had heard this information before, but coming from the Mounties, we trusted it as a confirmation that these beasts were not to be taken lightly.

"We have bear spray," I reminded them.

"Good," one said, "But you need to be no further than twenty feet away for that stuff to work, and you don't wanna be caught twenty feet from a polar bear. Take my word for it, avoid 'em at all costs."

As I pondered our chances of actually encountering a polar bear, a third officer walked in from the garage and set his hat on a desk. It was quite tidy throughout the station, so the hat looked out of place on the otherwise organized surface. It took a moment for me to notice that there was something wrong. The new officer looked flush and out of breath.

"There's a drunk kid at the high school with a shotgun," said the Mountie who had just entered.

I looked in horror at the other two, with whom I had been previously chatting.

"Another day in Oxford House," said one of them with a shake of his head, though a slight flash of anxiety flicked across the corner of his mouth. In the seclusion of the wild north, alcoholism was as rampant here as Norway House, or perhaps even worse.

"You need to get back to your canoe, right?" said the other, standing up and grabbing his own hat. "Why don't you hop in the car and we'll give you a lift on our way."

Back at the canoe, I thanked the Mounties and wished them luck on their school visit. They didn't seem to be worried, so I tried not to be either. Colton was back at Marvin's cabin across the street, meeting a local minister who used to be a trapper in the region. He was originally from Cleveland but moved to Norway House in his twenties and never left northern Manitoba. This country was interesting. For some, like our minister friend, the thrill and beauty of the untouched wilderness had a peace that ensnared them. For others, that same thrill and remoteness could destroy the humanity within, creating animals or worse out of once civilized men.

While packing our new groceries into the food pack, I noted the sort of supplies Colton had bought. Two bottles of Coke, two bags of Doritos, two chocolate brownies, a pizza-flavored convenience store hoagie, and an extra box of rice.

"What's all this?" I said. "I thought we needed more meals! You know, in case we get stranded and run out of food?"

"Well," said Colton, never one to back down from an argument, "since food is flown in here, this alone was all we could afford, and I really wanted the snacks. We need a morale boost, and the sandwich has like, five-thousand calories. That's a day's worth of food right there!"

He did get extra rice, and the brownies were too good to pass up. "Okay, you win," I said, cracking open my bottle of cola.

Oxford House sat at the outlet of the Hayes River from Oxford Lake, so it didn't take long before we were riding the current once again. The water was pristine. At one point, we looked down and the river was so clear that we felt the odd sensation of floating in midair, five feet above a sandy valley. The occasional weeds flowed with the current like prairie grass in the wind.

Frequent rapids soon littered the Hayes River beyond Oxford House, and we navigated through them with increasing confidence. Before reaching each set of fastwater, we would either pull ashore or stand in the canoe to scout the best route. Sometimes we were right, sometimes we were not. When we were wrong, the blue sky and warm breeze made the consequences feel less severe, and none of the rapids were as dangerous as the one that swamped us days before. Truth be told, the rush was gradually growing on me, and the constant activity made the afternoon fly by. Every now and then, we let out hollers of jubilation, to be so free to ride the current and drops with little shame. Suddenly, I wished for the trip to never end, for this moment to last forever. It was remarkable the psychological impact that sunny days with little wind held.

Near mid-day, we pulled over to a clear portage on the right side of the river. We had been able to hear the sound of water crashing on rock for a quarter mile, so we knew that Knife Rapids were near. A set of three violent falls, running these rapids would not be left up to the fate of a cracker flip. The well-traveled path, still not far from Oxford House, was evidence of the local fishing route.

At the head of the portage, I donned our cooking pack and abruptly heard a loud hissing noise.

"That's the gas!" I yelled.

I hurled the pack off my back and we sprinted down the path, far away from our gear. At what we felt was a safe distance, we paused to listen for a boom. When none came, we took a moment to think rationally.

"Why would the gas hiss?" contemplated Colton. "And even if it was the gas, why would it explode? It's not a bomb."

I thought about it and recognized he was right. In the absence of an open flame or spark, a leaking gas canister would have little consequence beyond its implications on the heating of our future meals. Feeling a bit sheepish, I quipped, "Better safe than sorry. Plus, you ran too!"

As we approached our packs to investigate, I attempted to look calm but noticed that Colton was equally apprehensive, which relieved my embarrassment significantly. The pack was resting peacefully upside down on the rocky shore, and we each paused ten feet away.

"You threw it, you open it," said Colton.

I smiled and stepped forward, knowing there was nothing to fear, yet feeling tense nonetheless. Pulling open the brown leather top, I immediately noticed a burning, acrid odor. It was surely not the gas, but instead smelt strongly of a spoiled poison. The scent alone was enough to make my eyes and nostrils burn.

"Colton," I said, shuffling bits of the gear carefully. "The can of bear spray went off."

He swore angrily under his breath.

"It's our cooking pack," I added redundantly.

Instead of cleaning it there, we opted to complete the trip to the other side of the falls and deal with it then. Feeling our heightened vulnerability to bears, we made an even stronger effort to keep a loud conversation going throughout the portage. Our insults continued to grow more malicious.

At the bottom of the rapids, we stared at the spectacle of rushing water for a moment. It mesmerized us like a bonfire on a cool summer night, but we both pondered silently how exactly we would clean what was essentially mace on steroids from our cooking gear. Standing still allowed us to notice the swarm of bugs who called this place home, so we decided to paddle out into the current and downstream a ways to escape. At a set of boulders in the middle of the channel, we pulled over, ate a chicken tortilla lunch, and finished off our snacks (Doritos and Coke) from that morning. After lunch, we finally set about cleaning the contents of the bear-spray-coated cooking pack.

The reaction was delayed and crept up on us slowly. A lone Canadian horsefly had managed to follow us from the end of Knife Rapids and took an interest in both of our faces as we cleaned. In the act of swatting away the fly, we each inadvertently touched our faces, eyes, and mouths. From there, as we scratched an itch, or rubbed our eyes, it grew exponentially. Initially, the skin on our hands and faces felt a dull warmth, as though sunburnt. Then our mouths began to tingle. Before we knew it, our eyes were swelling shut, and our throats burned from our mouths to stomachs.

The rotten scent of mace manifested itself in a taste that I thought would eliminate my appetite forever. As my eyes swelled over, my throat followed suit, restricting my breathing and sending me into a panic. Colton and I had foolishly thought that the dangerous oil in the mace could be simply rinsed off with water. While that was partially true (we had been able to remove a large volume of it), its insolubility and our lack of soap meant that the pain-causing remnants of it remained on everything. The warning label on the back of the canister read "Dangerous: This product will cause extreme eye and respiratory irritation if direct contact or ingestion occurs. Seek immediate medical attention." Our worst fears coming to fruition, we were officially in trouble.

CHAPTER 13

Out of Range

Our hearts raced as our lungs struggled. I pulled our map onto the packs between us in the canoe. Colton spun in the bow and contorted his body towards it to get a clear view. We scanned the map, frantically looking for somewhere downstream that could help us. Paddling back up the Hayes, especially given the dozens of rapids that we had negotiated down that afternoon, was not an option. The Mounties had warned me that they wouldn't be able to do emergency evacuations close to Hudson Bay, but we certainly weren't that far out yet. I considered the consequences of an evacuation. Aside from the cost, it would likely end the trip. Also not an option.

I tried to stay calm. Surely exposure to bear spray on its own would not do any permanent damage. It must just be painful. Extraordinarily painful. With each moment that I reassured myself, the stinging and swelling got worse, and my confidence in our immediate safety weakened. If it did do serious damage to our eyesight, or somehow poison us, this was the worst place on Earth for that to happen.

"The settlement at God's Lake is about fifty miles from us," Colton pointed out. God's River was the route that Sevareid and Port had taken eighty-three years prior when the Hayes, their planned route, was unnavigable due to low water levels. It was a longer route that veered east of ours, not far after the Echimamish River. God's Lake was larger than Oxford Lake, with the God's River flowing in and out from west to east.

"That's as the crow flies," I added. "I don't see a direct route either, so it would be a couple of days' paddle."

"Crap."

"Hey, what about this?" I pointed to the map, at a spot on Knee Lake. The shape of an "S," Knee Lake spans almost forty miles from the southwest entrance to the northeast end, where the Hayes River flows out. We currently sat only a mile from the southwest corner of the lake and traversing it was a part of our planned route. I was pointing to something that we had not yet noticed in the southern end of the "S" – a small airstrip connected to an unmarked, windy road on a south-facing peninsula.

"Probably an abandoned town." Neither of us had heard of a settlement here, but maps don't lie.

"It's our only shot."

"Agreed."

It was 5:30 PM and the town was about fifteen miles away. Knowing we had to hurry, as navigating this lake in the dark with impeded vision wasn't ideal, we left immediately.

We have never paddled faster. It helped that the lake's surface was glass in the windless evening. Despite the panic, I visualized waterskiing on these unspoiled waters. Its familiarity was comforting.

As we neared our target, I thought I heard the sound of a distant engine. Our map was telling the truth. Even more, the town was inhabited!

We arrived a little more than two hours after departing the falls. The tiny airstrip and roads, it turned out, did not service a town, though our guess wasn't far off. North Star Resort, a fly-in fishing company, owned the land. Apparently, some things had changed along the historic Hayes River route. We necessarily welcomed this unexpected bit of civilization, and they generously brought us in with open arms. The employees took pity on our situation and allowed us to wash off in their bathroom sinks. Running water – what a joy! We did our best to rinse out our singed eyes and scorched mouths, but the workers assured us that only time would fully calm the pain, adding that the bear spray wouldn't do permanent damage. "Just hurts like the dickens for a while."

Talking to a group of employees during our dinner on the front lawn, they informed us that this winter had been extraordinarily late. In fact, only ten days prior, they had been driving trucks on the lake's ice. Despite this, business was good, and the guests had every cabin booked full. Truly dedicated anglers care little of temperature or comfort, though the thirty horsepower motors on their boats and warm cabins each night undoubtedly sweetened the deal a bit.

"Ever been through the rapids section or beyond?" asked Colton. We had yet to meet someone who had and were eager to hear a first-hand account.

"Nope," one said. He was younger, in his mid-twenties, and had a clean-shaven face. I suspected that by the end of the summer, he would hardly be recognizable. Perhaps the comfy lifestyle of resort living tempered the typical wear and tear on the body that the Canadian bush would otherwise cause. "Heard of a few who've done it, not many, though, and you'll definitely be the first this year. I hear the weather gets pretty harsh by the bay too, and you need to watch out for polar bears."

We were beginning to notice a common theme in the locals' words of wisdom. Without our bear spray, though, "watching out" seemed a tad futile. "Hoping" was now our best bet.

After dinner, we set up our tent near shore and retired early. There was still light shining mildly through the tent wall as we wrapped ourselves in our sleeping bags, finishing off the brownies that Colton had purchased that morning in Oxford House. He was right, we did need a morale boost. We convinced ourselves to finish them all, justified by the fact that they would be perfect bear bait as we continued deeper into the remote wilderness beyond. To be safe, we ate crumbs off the tent floor, at least half of which were brownie, the other half dirt, creating an enticing new recipe. We couldn't risk being sniffed out by a hungry bear, after all, so we enjoyed eating the concoction for good measure.

We arose early on the lawn of the North Star Resort and were on our way. The burning sensations had re-appeared overnight, indicating that time alone would indeed be the only cure. Our eyes and throats felt, at least, a little bit better.

The northern and southern sections of the "S" of Knee Lake point northeast, generally towards York Factory. From the resort, Colton and I traveled along the southern section until the lake took a sharp turn to the north, where a six-mile stretch of open water scattered with dozens of islands would connect us to the larger north section.

Somewhere in this connecting body of water lies Magnetic Island, known for its unique composition, a material that we were warned might lead our compasses awry. Perhaps part rural legend, we debated the story's merits so emphatically that before we knew it, we ourselves were lost. Despite regular warnings and our generally constant attention, it had only happened once or twice throughout the entire trip. This time, though, seemed more serious. We knew that we needed to head north, and that there was only one outlet from the middle section of Knee Lake, but the legend led us to mistrust our compass. The sea of islands looked identical from our vantage, masterfully disguising themselves as mainland, so that locating the outlet seemed unlikely at best. We could be lost for days.

Within minutes of losing our place, we jubilantly cheered the passing of three fishing boats with the North Star Resort emblem painted on their aluminum bows. Mistaking our cheers for waves, they smiled back and tipped their caps, unaware they had saved us many hours of panic.

We followed the path of the fishing boats to the outlet, which led to the north arm of Knee Lake. With another exchange of pleasantries at the narrows, this time in closer quarters, we passed the last bit of human contact until Hudson Bay and aimed our craft northeast. At last, we were on our own.

Knowing the weather forecast was glum, we relished the sixty-degree temperatures and made swift progress across the vast, final twenty miles of big-lake paddling. Our bronzed torsos soaked in the sun and a slight breeze warded off any trace of Canadian bugs from the open water.

It turned out the bugs were just biding their time. After Knee Lake, the Hayes River reemerged with force. Warm temperatures over the last couple of days had been ideal hatching conditions for mosquitos, who, back in the windless river, attacked without mercy.

Quickly, we found Canadian mosquitos different from those in Minnesota. Both of us had been under the impression that growing up in the land of lakes and bloodsuckers, we would be well trained for any bugs that dared come our way. We were misguided. Instead of the bulky, irritable mosquitos from home, these nasty devils swarmed like gnats, in clouds of millions, on occasion literally blocking out the sun. Dusk had arrived, which was ideal feeding time, and we were fresh meat.

As the Hayes River resumed its descent, it split into several channels, all equally rapid-laden according to the map. With no other way to decide, we played a three-way, round-robin style tournament of flipping the compass. The westernmost route won with an undefeated record.

Through tiny channels that hardly fit our canoe, over ledges and around sharp bends, we recklessly charged downstream like the log flume ride at Six Flags. If we were to stop, the mosquitos would surely win. At least if we tipped, the water would protect us from their miniature but toxic stingers.

Almost to Swampy Lake, we approached a set of non-negotiable rapids, even in Colton's ambitious eyes. We would have to portage. The only problem: as we paddled north from Knee Lake, the landscape around us had morphed from a thick pine forest into a recently demolished burn-site, littered with millions of dead, smoldered trees. As far as the eye could see, our surroundings were a barren wasteland. Blocking what used to be the portage trail were hundreds of fallen trees, their branches jutting out in all directions. We surmised that the burn had taken place the previous autumn, as ashes were scarce, and the trail had yet to be cleared. It wasn't as though we expected the Canadian Park Service to be maintaining the portages of this region, but if somebody had come through before us, the trail would have, optimally, been cleared out to some minimal extent. There was some consolation in knowing that at least the next group through would have an easier go of it.

It took nearly an hour to make our way through the brush and fallen pine. Mosquitos amplified the difficulty, swarming our faces and kamikaze diving into our eyes. I had to squint just to avoid them, and each time one made it through my defenses, I instinctively rubbed it away with my bear-spray-ridden hands. We were paying a dear price for our luck so far, lacking a significant interaction throughout the trip with these winged beasts. The dismal paddling conditions had kept the bugs away until now, and I couldn't decide which I preferred.

Cutting the portage short (we were hardly sure that we were even on the portage), the two of us hopped back into the canoe. In doing so, we inadvertently got in over our heads, chaotically smashing our way through the set's remaining rapids. Traveling sideways down the current at one point, I looked down to see a huge boulder just below the water's surface. I braced for impact, preparing to submerge in the recently ice-covered river. Miraculously, the canoe floated over the rock untouched, clearing it by what had to be millimeters. One more pound of cargo weighing us down and the trip might have ended right there.

Falling over one final three-foot ledge, we landed in a calm pool, still surrounded by the burnt down forest. Most everything looked grey, but there were definite signs of new life, and it was clear that the burn did not hit this area as hard. A sparse grouping of untouched, mature trees lined the water's edge.

On the right was an open space with tall grass growing along a rounded peninsula. Beyond this small point was Swampy Lake, and then the rapids section: forty straight miles of rapids before its finale, White Mud Falls. One hundred sixty miles in all left to York Factory. It was a deceiving number, as they would be the most grueling of the trip. Here we camped (not before completing a full forty-yard dash into the tent to lose our tailing bugs), thankful to be alive and dry. The unrelenting buzz of mosquitos on our tent's screen door serenaded us to sleep.

Day 46 - June 12, 2008 – Beginning of the "Rapids Section"

"Right!" I yelled at the top of my lungs from the front of our speeding canoe, switching the paddle to my left side and stroking with all my might.

On the spot, our canoe turned sharply to the right, narrowly avoiding a boulder hiding just below the surface. It zipped by harmlessly, allowing my eyes to refocus on the next obstacle ahead. We were heading at a forty-five-degree angle towards the stone shoreline, so I switched my paddle hands yet again, this time to the right side. *Was that shore? Perhaps it was another island; it was impossible to tell anymore.*

"Paddle hard right!" shouted Colton from the stern.

I was distracted. Attempting to decipher the landscape had blinded me to a rock, this time sticking several feet out of the water, thirty feet ahead and nearing fast.

Colton swung the canoe back to the left, now facing straight down the river. Our rightward momentum, though, continued to drift us toward the rock, now just ten feet away.

"Brace for impact!" I shouted back, continuing to paddle on the right until the last second, narrowly avoiding a snapped paddle and smashed hand.

There was no missing this one. Instinctively, we both leaned hard away from the rock, knowing that the impact would tip us to the right. Our lean worked. With a loud crunch, our canoe bounced off intact and upright, and continued to float downriver.

No time to rest, not just yet. Forty feet ahead, the water came to a straight, horizontal line. We knew what this meant: waterfalls. I looked left, then right, then left again, searching for a "V" in the water ripples, indicating a sloped path. Finding these V-shaped routes was our goal in rapids, as they generally indicated a passage clear of rocks and ledges.

There were none in sight. Forty feet quickly turned to thirty, then twenty. It was difficult to tell how big the falls were; perhaps anywhere from two to four feet. The former would be doable; the latter, extremely risky. In a last-ditch effort to find a pass, I stood up, hoping to provide my eyes a better vantage point. Sure enough, I spotted a "V" just to our left.

"Colton," I called back, "five feet to the left!"

Fighting my instinct, I paddled yet again with all my strength as Colton performed a masterful maneuver, guiding the craft safely through the fortunately small drop.

I rested my oar sideways over my lap and leaned forward, staring at my feet in disgust. A simple, millisecond lapse in concentration had almost led to disaster. Not only did I almost ruin the trip, but we knew full well that a wrecked canoe in these parts could likely end our lives.

"My bad with that rock, bud; I don't know what happened," I said hollowly.

"It wasn't even that bad. Kind of fun, actually!" He was trying to cheer me up. I recognized his attempt at humor and appreciated the gesture. It would have been easy, with our stress near breaking point, for Colton to jab an insult at me. No doubt, a small part of him surely wanted to.

"Thanks." I looked ahead to where the river inevitably led us. "Well, I'll be sure to make it up during this set," I said, standing up calmly. "More rapids a hundred yards away."

Our entire morning consisted of this. We would finish a rapid having paddled through with several close calls, followed by lining an un-maneuverable portion, and then hop back in the canoe for more twists and turns. Then, another hundred yards after the last one, we would start the routine all over again. After only limited practice, it didn't take long for us each to master the art of scouting and running whitewater.

We knew ahead of time from Hap Wilson's maps that much of the rapids section would be characterized by a jumbled maze of mid-rapid islands and forks in the river. What we didn't know was that many of these so-called "forks" had, in themselves, many more forks, the river braiding as many as five or six strands. Within no time, we lost our location on the zoomed out map. An absence of relevant landmarks prevented us from discerning where we were, so each rapid looked much the same as the rest. It seemed troubling at first to be without bearings, but upon realizing that as long as we continued to paddle downstream and stay alive, we would end up at Hudson Bay one way or the other.

Lunch in the rapids section was a rather difficult ordeal. For a while, we attempted to find a spot with a suitable area to cook, but eventually conceded to a mossy, fifteen-foot cliff with a three-foot-wide ledge halfway up. It was as good a spot as any, really, and with a stove-heated chicken wrap, we might as well have been royalty. Despite the cold drizzle that had persisted all day, the soft moss was a comfortable seat, and the sound of rushing water nearly soothed me to sleep.

After lunch, Colton now in the bow and me back to the stern, the whitewater continued at an alarming rate. One set of rapids we came upon held an island in the middle with a clearly un-manageable set of falls to the right. On the left was a smaller ledge, capable of lining down, with a drop of average difficulty directly after. Our choice was clear.

Just before the initial ledge, on the island side of the left rapids, we pulled onto a downed tree and Colton climbed out, all the while holding a firm grip on the rope tied to the front of the canoe. Next, I crawled onto the tree, which stuck out over the murderous rapids, guiding the back of our vessel around the low hanging branches, and then over the subsequent ledge. Without a choice in the matter, I continued to inch ever closer to the tree's tip; I needed to get our rig past its obstructer. The weakened tree groaned, lurching downward as I neared the end, before suddenly giving way. With a sharp inhale, I dropped violently into the icy whitewater.

Instantly, my mind and body went numb. A grey cloud filled my brain and I forgot where I was. I opened my eyes to find myself chest deep, floating in a set of rapids, grasping for dear life to a rope in my left hand and the feeble branches of a fallen tree in my right. I couldn't remember how I got there, and it was miraculous that my hands had found the energy to hold on, as my muscles were unwilling to do my bidding at all.

With a glance at Colton's face, I understood the gravity of our situation. He displayed a look of sheer horror and helpless dismay, mouth ajar at a loss for words. The water wasn't cold, to me. In fact, the temperature of my surroundings was the last thing on my mind, not even reaching the threshold of thought. All I could focus on was getting my paralyzed body to respond. To make any movement... any movement would do.

Without my recognition, Colton had taken action, now lying head-first towards me on the remains of the fallen tree, his arm outstretched, reaching, begging, demanding my attention.

"Grab my arm!" he yelled, attempting to snap me out of my daze.

I stared at his hand. The water on his neoprene glove shined like icicles despite the foggy afternoon. The typical synaptic process of thought leading to action was failing. Simply telling my brain to grab his hand did nothing. Instead, I had to focus on the act of moving at all.

"Take my hand!" His voice was haggard with anguish.

First a finger.

Then, the hand.

Finally, I found the strength to move my arm as a whole.

With my left hand, so as to not let go of the tree, I reached for Colton's arm. It took several tries; I couldn't let go of the rope connecting me to the canoe either, and the weight of the water trying to drag it downstream tore the muscles in my chest down the center. If Colton were to save me, but we lost the canoe in the process, it would be useless. We would certainly perish. Death flashed across my brain. This would not be it; it could not. It was not only my life on the line here. Without me, the rest of the rapids section would be beyond perilous for Colton alone. Of course he could send out a rescue call with our SPOT messenger, assuming he recovered the gear, but it would take days for them to come, surely longer than it would take for hypothermia to set in.

With a desperate reach and holler, our hands connected, and along with the rope in our grasp, he pulled me to his portion of the tree and dragged me up. For a moment, we sat in silence, breathing heavily and attempting to comprehend exactly what just happened.

He had saved my life, and forever that would be between us.

"Thanks," I muttered. It was all I could muster.

"Don't mention it," he responded simply. "You must be freezing. Let's get you into a space blanket."

"I'm okay, really." I wasn't trying to be tough. My body truly felt fine, or I was in shock, but all that I wanted was to continue forward, to keep moving. "Let's just keep going; the exercise will keep me warm."

Ironically, the whole ordeal had occurred during what was

supposed to be an easy part of running rapids. Generally, lining was the safer option when facing a dangerous stretch, intended to be a more controllable means of getting down whitewater. The bit of rapids remaining would be far from stress-free, and we both knew it. Fear, however, could not be a part of our vocabulary, no matter how much we actually felt it. We knew that the second fear became verbalized, there was no turning back. It would engulf us, making almost every task from here on out seem exponentially more daunting. It was already time to move on.

Holding our canoe as still as possible in the swift current below the ledge, still standing on the tree, we scouted the scene ahead. We were in an awkward position. The only way out was to start with the canoe broadside to the river, despite a large rock lying just downstream from the stern, and a three-foot waterfall just below the bow. Our only option was to, upon jumping in, let the current take the boat for a split second towards the drop until the stern cleared the boulder, at which point we would cut sharply to the left to avoid the ledge. We would be threading a needle, and largely at the mercy of the current. If it were to carry us in some unforeseen way, there would be trouble.

On the count of three we hopped in, pushed off, and waited for the current to catch hold. Colton, in the front, began paddling on the right side to give the current a helping hand. I, on the other hand, was required to be poised and ready to make the turn to the left. As usual, nature treated us to a surprise. Instead of carrying the craft towards the small drop, the current pushed us directly towards the rock below the stern. In one fell swoop, we became wedged between the rock and the flow of heavy rapids. With the boulder and canoe acting as a sort of teeter-totter, I was sure that the current would pivot us around the rock and into the opposite direction than expected: backwards.

"Turn around!" I yelled. As we had done on several occasions before, I turned in my seat and knelt on the floor of the canoe, taking my position as bow-master.

Colton disagreed. Confident that the current would still direct us as planned, he stood his ground, causing us both to paddle in the opposite direction at the same time. We sat stalled there until finally

Colton turned around, accepting the stern position. He did so, however, simultaneously with my decision to rotate back towards him. In what would have been more fitting on a dance floor, our spinning jarred free the canoe from its position. Once loose, we matched our directions and maneuvered the rest of the way down routinely.

At the bottom, we looked back at what seemed from the lower side to be nothing more than a mediocre set of fast water. There had been many narrow escapes on our trip, but the last ten minutes would be, we hoped, the closest experience to death and disaster either of us would ever face. I shivered; the adrenaline was fading away to reveal my soaked legs and torso.

My thoughts drifted momentarily to the days of fur traders, traveling up the Hayes River from York Factory to Norway House in York boats, elongated vessels that more closely resembled Viking ships than canoes. Their sturdy frames were more durable in whitewater, especially when compared to the birch bark canoes of old, and they were capable of carrying substantial loads as far west as the Rocky Mountains. While they were typically manned by up to a dozen traders, the prospect of attempting to climb the rapids section upstream, no matter the craft, sent further chills down my spine.

"You ready?" Colton called back.

I looked up. Colton was standing at the bow, staring another hundred yards in front, scouting the best line to take through the next rocky rollercoaster. Fog rested ominously throughout the river valley, rising and sinking in swifts where the current was strongest. Life on the Hayes River.

CHAPTER 14

The Battle of the Hayes

Rain spattered the hood of my raincoat, careening outward off the brim before falling to the frosted ground. The permafrost shores of the North Atlantic Ocean reaches south to stretches of the Hayes River. Of course, the ground isn't frozen on the surface, but several feet below the muddy base, the soil remains solid.

Above the frozen mud, the tundra surrounding the Hayes River is covered in a spongy plant called sphagnum, or peat moss. Common throughout boggy wetlands in the Northern Hemisphere, peat moss does wonders for the environment and local ecosystems but made land-navigation for Colton and me a living nightmare.

When the rain fell from my hood, it didn't splash off the ground like usual, nor did it run quickly into the river that lay just below my feet. Instead, it soaked into the moss, disappearing like snakes in grass. The moss looked firm enough to support me, but my intuition said otherwise.

We were at the start of a half-kilometer portage around an enormous waterfall, the largest of the rapids section. The entrance to the trail was nearly invisible, especially through the misty fog, so we were fortunate to have found it before getting too close to the deadly drop.

With one foot resting barely on shore and the other still in the canoe, I donned one pack onto my back, and then the other to my front. Taking the first step onto the mossy path, I regretted immediately my choice years ago to sacrifice a clear view of my feet for the luxury of not carrying our canoe. As accustomed to double packing as I was, this trail was hell-bent on making my life difficult.

"Alright?" Colton asked as I tiptoed in a semi-circle to face him. Every move I made had to be with the most deliberate intention to avoid falling from the uneven, mashed-potato-like ground. To be honest, I wasn't sure I would be able to get back up if I fell.

"I'm alright," I lied. "Need help lifting the canoe?" My voice was doing its best to sound genuinely helpful, but between us, an unspoken passive aggressiveness that can only be found in true Minnesotans was smoldering. We each knew how much the mental and physical wear was tearing us down, but admitting so would be to admit defeat to the other. The two of us had come this far together, but our enthusiastic teamwork was gradually shifting into a silent competition of will. Outright jabs and insults were off the table, so we were left with a drive to be the stronger of the two. We weren't far from the location where Port and Severeid had come to blows, and while they patched together their friendship long enough to reach Hudson Bay alive, the final two hundred miles of Canadian bush did irreparable damage to their relationship. Perhaps passive aggressiveness was the way to go after all.

Colton shook his head and picked up the canoe, placing it over his shoulders. He gave me a nod to indicate that he was ready, and off we went into the dark forest ahead, traveling at snail speed to secure our footing. With every step we sank knee-deep into the moss, each time ominously clung to by the thick, stinking material. Then, with a wet slap like a moist suction cup, our foot released and moved forward, on to its next step.

We counted our staggered paces to determine when to take breaks along the hike, adding them out loud as our bear deterrent. Continuing our tradition of insults to scare unwanted wildlife was risky business; I expected it would soon go too far. Counting seemed safer. In the nine-mile Grand Portage the year previous, which connected us from the Pigeon River to Lake Superior, and concluded our Border Trip, we rested every three hundred steps. The extra energy required in order to proceed through the peat moss was taking its toll, however, so we were forced to switch to one hundred steps. Each break consisted of a resounding sigh as we dropped our gear, a couple minutes of silence, and then a mutual look and head nod, indicating that it was time to continue. Two minutes was all it took for our perpetually soaked bodies to shiver again, so the motivation to continue hiking was strong.

Towards the end of the portage rushed a stream, perpendicular to the trail, and only one skimpy log remained of a bridge that appeared to have once provided travelers safe passage across. The stream wasn't intimidating by any means, only ten feet wide and two feet deep. However, it was deeper than we would've liked to wade, and much too wide to jump. A brief survey of the neighboring area indicated a surprising lack of downed trees, and we concluded that our best option was to attempt to use the one-tree bridge, hoping that it would hold under our weight.

While crossing, I tried to look down to the stream below, just as movies warn their most balance-deficient characters not to do in these situations. Of course, the pack around my stomach prevented me from fully committing the cardinal sin, but being able to see my feet would have been beneficial. The limb was predictably slippery, and my boots were hardly meant for balancing on logs. After two steps, I abandoned the "slow and steady" plan and made a run for it. At my final step, my left foot slid out from under me, and I performed a spectacular *deboule en manege* onto the opposite bank, landing awkwardly onto my side. The spin would have scored me a ten, but the fall might have rendered me disqualified. I flung mud from my sleeves as my two-packed self resettled onto my feet, determined to complete the final hundred paces with dignity.

As the day neared its close, beyond our eventual completion of the portage from hell, we approached a set of rapids with which no safe path could be found. Thirty yards before their start, we pulled to the left shore to scout from higher ground. Walking along the rocky shore, I paused, grasping the weak branches that hung over the river, and thought fearfully of my experience earlier that day. I prayed that these branches would hold.

No safe passage down the rapids could be found.

Back at the canoe, we started through the brush and eventually found a trail that followed the river to the opposite end of the rapids. Luck, this time, was on our side. Thankfully, we would not have to blunder through another peat bog.

We decided that this would be the end of our day, despite the fact that it was far from dusk. Darkness, we were finding, was tough to come by, and without sundown as a warning, 10:00 PM snuck up on us.

In a lazy attempt to discourage bears from finding our tent site, we set up camp at the high side of the portage and carried the rest of our gear, food included, to the opposite end, downstream of the rapids. Here we sat on our upside-down canoe for dinner, bundled in rain gear, only our eyes visible to the outside world. Rain poured down ruthlessly, causing our cold tortilla sandwiches to grow soggy within minutes.

After the meal, I stared for a while at the lonely river, drifting by innocently. The rain turned into a breezy mist as it fell on my exposed hands. Fog blocked the opposite shore from view. Somehow, I began to laugh.

"What?" Colton asked. We had been silent for some time now.

"If only our friends could see us now," I replied with a smile. "I mean, we're constantly miserable, constantly hungry, and constantly wet. And it's all by choice!"

Colton chuckled. "Yeah, I suppose it was our choice."

We were to the point that it no longer felt like we were taking this trip on our own accord. It was a mission, and we had to do it. Upon reflection, though, it didn't seem such a chore after all.

"You know, despite everything," he said, "we're still having the time of our lives."

I smiled in agreement. We hiked back through the dripping forest to our tent, this time with a bit of a hop in our step. *Almost there.*

Fog and mist lingered into our second day of the Rapids Section, and I had the strong inkling that it would be with us for the remainder of our voyage. We had heard of the infamous Hudson Bay fog, and despite remaining over one hundred thirty miles from York Factory, we were certain that we were experiencing it in the flesh.

From the rapids that we had camped by the night before, it was approximately a half day's paddle to White Mud Falls. Before White Mud, the rapids became sparser and less treacherous.

As seems to be the case with wilderness travel, though, a false sense of security can prove to be disastrous. At a set of rapids just before White Mud, carelessness nearly caused catastrophe. What we had initially thought would be a tame riffle based on our memory of the map's markings revealed its truly tumultuous nature just fifty feet away.

"Hear that? Falls ahead!" called Colton.

Noticing the distinct difference in the sound of the upcoming falls relative to that of typical rapids, Colton stood from the bow to confirm his observation. It took all of two seconds to do so, dropping like a bullet back down to his chair.

"Definitely a waterfall." His face was blue.

We were now thirty feet from the disastrous plummet, so we veered sharply to the shore on the right. Unable to leap out onto land due to its steep incline, Colton clawed fiercely at the tree roots that jutted from the bank, securing our position in the process. We came in from an angle, and his grasp upon shore allowed the canoe to continue its pivot under us, the stern and me swinging out into the river before coming to rest, facing upstream. The incline, now on our left, was severe enough to prevent us from portaging on this side.

Facing upstream, it turned out, would be helpful, as we now needed to ferry the canoe across the river, hopefully landing at a mid-falls rock island. We would portage down from there. The art of ferrying is simple enough in theory, but puts one's paddling abilities to a real test. Essentially, you act as if you are trying to paddle upstream rather than across it, angling just slightly towards your desired shore. When executed properly, it should appear as a slow traversing of the river's breadth. We pushed off, continuing to face upstream, paddling with all our might. In current this strong, just above a falls, even the strongest paddlers in the world would have their nerve tested, fighting to move each inch forward.

Looking over my shoulder, I saw the falls approaching rapidly. I yelped in terror, which caused Colton to look back as well.

"No time!" I barked. "We're losing too much ground!"

Traditionally when ferrying, the bowman paddles on the side you are aiming for, keeping the craft pointed generally upstream, while the stern man paddles on the other side, angling the canoe ever so slightly towards the destination. With twenty feet between us and the waterfall, I made a split-second decision. Nearing the island, I defied the rules in a moment of panic and called out, "Switch to the left!"

Colton switched without argument. Second guessing decisions in rapids can be disastrous. He switched, and the canoe turned on a dime to the right, swinging the bow straight towards the island. We were too close to the edge, fifteen feet from the drop. We weren't going to make it. My paddle whirled like the blades of a helicopter.

In one motion, Colton seized the bow-rope and leaped for safety, paddle still in hand. His trailing right foot caught the river and sent a mirror of glassy water into the mist while his left foot drew solid footing, able to scramble onto shore. Colton rolled to face me, and from his bottom he wedged each foot against the rocks, bracing for the rope to go taut in his hands. The canoe's stern, myself aboard, swept ever-closer to the falls, eventually hanging directly over the ledge. I knew Colton would be able to hold on. If he couldn't, I was gone.

After what seemed like eons of suspense, the canoe lurched. Colton anchored the weight of our rig, my body, and my life in place. He reeled us in, hand over hand, away from the falls. Safely on shore, neither of us spoke, knowing what had nearly just occurred. It was the second time in as many days that he saved my life. The score in the "Battle of the Hayes" was Colton: 2 - Hayes River: 0.

In past moments of the trip where tensions were high, or when danger was narrowly avoided, we would laugh together, making light of the situation. This time, we did not. Perhaps the stakes were finally real, and we understood the gravity of where we were. Instead, I gave Colton a grim smile, patted his shoulder, and got to work unpacking for the portage. It was too cold to linger, and White Mud Falls was too near to rest. We paddled on.

Reaching White Mud was something of a milestone. Surrounding a small island with a few sparse pines were two sets of falls that dropped at least fifteen feet. It was not the sunny, glamorous moment that I had envisioned, but that hardly mattered. After sweeping the portage down the sloped rock, we each ate one granola bar for sustenance and another for celebration, as we sat and relaxed for ten short minutes. I should have been more excited. The rapids section, a character who repeatedly threatened our lives, had finally succumbed. In good weather, the final one hundred twenty miles ahead would be smooth sailing, but we were just behind winter. Noticing the harsh landscape before us, I could hardly allow myself to celebrate.

As we pushed into the now rapid-less river, we calculated out the remainder of our route. It was just after 10:00 AM, and the confluence with the God's River was sixty miles away. The hope was to make it there by nightfall, camp, and then finish the final sixty miles to the bay the following day. This fit perfectly with our desire to avoid landing too close to York Factory and its polar bear territory, so my mind was temporarily eased. While the man-eating bears were masterful swimmers, we at least *felt* more secure on water.

The current seemed to strengthen on the river's final descent after White Mud Falls, and our spirits were uplifted. Based on our view of the shore zooming past, we estimated ourselves traveling at seven, maybe even eight miles per hour. By now, we considered our eyes to be quite accurate speedometers. There was a slight head wind, but the riverbanks surrounding us had grown to over fifty feet tall and were laden with thick pines, so it could hardly reach us.

Every so often, we passed a clearing on the banks where pines gave way to empty clay, stripped with ruts all the way up to the top. They appeared at first to be remnants of winter avalanches, but before long, we recognized that they were mudslides. The frozen ground below the surface evidently resulted in unstable soil.

Just before lunch, we stumbled across something Colton had been looking for since day one: a souvenir. On the right bank, half buried in clay and snow, was a moose carcass, surely a victim of the recent winter. Rid of the majority of its skin and fur, the moose's bones jutted out from the ground like an unearthed graveyard, though clearly too large to be of human origin. After some convincing from

Colton, I pulled over so that he could remove the antlers and bring them with. With our food knife, he cut off the rack at the weakest point of the skeleton: the moose's neck.

I could smell the beast from the canoe as I held on to shore, my paddle jammed deep into the muck. Partially laughing and partially annoyed, I commented to Colton about his clouded vision and failure to accept the fact that we were about to add to our outfit the most potent piece of bear bait possible. Desperately, I hoped that he wouldn't manage to pry the antlers off. Sure enough, with a loud snap, the head and rack came clean off from the rest of the body, Colton tumbling backwards with a resounding thud onto the frozen bank, surprised by his prize's abrupt release.

"Come help me grab this," Colton called to me, a crazy smile across his face.

"You're joking," I said. "That thing reeks!"

"Yeah, but think about how great it would be to have this back home."

"If we get eaten by a polar bear, I'm going to kill you," I said back, reluctantly pulling the canoe further onto shore and getting out. Together, we placed the rack and still-connected skull onto the top of our already tattered spray skirt. For about half an hour, we continued to paddle, myself trailing in the horrid smell of rotting moose carcass. Finally having enough, I demanded an early lunch break so we could switch positions in the canoe.

We pulled to shore only to exchange seats, pushing back into the river with our food pack open for service. Eating lunch in the canoe was surprisingly relaxing; we could eat and make progress all at once. Even after lunch, our mood was, despite the cold and fog, quite positive. At this pace, we ambitiously anticipated the current assisting us to the bay by late night.

Like a bee to honey, within just an hour of adding the bait to our canoe, we found the most exotic wildlife of the trip. First, high above us on the top of the left bank, stood a cow moose and her two calves. As though they knew of the crime that we had committed, giving their fellow moose such an improper burial, the mother and children stood their ground, staring at us menacingly. Despite moose being more aggressive than many know, we weren't foolish enough to be frightened, as we were more than one hundred feet away, and were not between the cow and her young. Nonetheless, I hoped she would never in her right mind abandon them to chase a mysterious object like us down the river.

Bizarrely, only minutes after our encounter with the moose family, we came across a lonely black bear waddling along the right side water's edge. While it took us until we were quite close to the moose to see them, we noticed the bear when it was still several hundred yards in the distance and walking away. With the wind in our faces, we knew the beast couldn't smell us. She meandered along slowly, feet from shore, her snout down sifting through the mud, hunting for insects. The sheer wildness of the experience was enough to elevate our heartbeats. As we drew nearer, I could feel the clock ticking quickly before the bear would see us and run. Sure enough, no nearer than one hundred yards, she halted abruptly, lifted her nose to the sky, and snapped her enormous head towards us. For a split-second, I thought she would charge, but that was all. The next second, she bolted for the woods, halfway up the bank. As we thought about it, there was a strong possibility that we would be the first and last human interactions in any of these animals' lives. We were the intruders in *their* territory.

As the afternoon progressed, our confidence in the pace we were traveling lessened dramatically. We had projected ourselves to hit the confluence of the Fox River, thirty miles upstream from the God's River, and where the waterway doubles in size, within only a few hours of leaving White Mud Falls. This proved to be a massive overestimation of our abilities.

Every bend in the river seemed to be identical; if I didn't know any better, I would have thought we were traveling in circles. Each time we passed a bend, we built up in our minds that it would be the confluence of the Fox River. There, the river would open up and the current would double in speed; the picture was beautiful. Every bend that failed to materialize this image into reality tore away a piece of my heart, sending me into a demoralized mode of concern. Colton instead vocalized his frustration, shouting into the mist with each failed corner.

By the time we finally did hit the Fox River, the rain had reappeared and the wind blistered freely through the broad valley. After building it up in my head, the confluence was nothing as I had imagined. At the moment the Fox and Hayes Rivers meet, the landscape transforms. The maximum height of trees gradually shrinks and the tall banks become essentially bare. No longer surrounded by a lush green forest, brown and grey filled our surroundings. In this vacant land, wind was open to gust for miles, threatening anything that stuck out against the cold surface.

We took a break at the confluence, once again without pulling to shore. In spite of the current, after five minutes, we hadn't moved an inch, except perhaps backwards. The wind, having been blocked before now by the smaller river and wooded landscape, felt gale-force.

"This is unbelievable!" I yelled. The howling squall sounded like a jet engine roaring past our ears.

Colton nodded wordlessly, then moved his mouth out from behind his fully zipped raincoat. "Shall we?"

Back on our way, the wind whipped our faces and stirred the current, creating whitecaps of nearly two feet in height. There was a definite coldness to the new river valley. It felt dead. Temperatures were below freezing, certainly, but the coldness was more than that. We were astronauts on the moon, and there wasn't a soul within tens or perhaps hundreds of miles. The desolate landscape screamed inhospitable, like we were insulting it for even thinking we could travel through unscathed. We had tempted fate throughout the rapids section, and fate was going to have the last word.

As we battled on, the mist that had defined the previous couple of days had changed into a windy sleet, having adjusted to the now sub-freezing temperature. Our faces burned with pain as the icy pellets scratched at our flesh, forcing us to cover every exposed scrap of skin besides the eyes. To my great fortune, I was currently in the bow and was in no way required to use my vision. Colton was not so lucky. I turtled my head into my coat and embraced the blindness while Colton led us forward.

The score in the "Battle of the Hayes" was Colton: 2 - Hayes River: 1.

CHAPTER 15

This Place is Death

We were paddling blind. As was the case in the rapids, our progress was a mystery. Our tolerance for staying calm and mindlessly plodding on, based solely on the knowledge that as long as we continued downstream, we would make it to Hudson Bay, was increasingly slim. By 10:00 PM, though the sky was as bright as noon, we knew that night was upon us, as was the time for us to make a decision. First, we had to find ourselves on the map. The use of our hands for this task was difficult, considering their sensation was completely gone, but we managed to surmise that we were still fifteen miles from the God's River confluence, and seventy-five from York Factory.

We were advised not to camp between the God's River and York Factory, but if the current wind continued, it was doubtful we would be able to make the full sixty miles in one day. This left three options: paddle through the night tonight and hopefully be able to stave off sleep and cold until reaching York Factory, paddle the fifteen miles to the confluence tonight and then hopefully be able to paddle the remaining sixty miles tomorrow, or call it quits right then, paddle thirty miles tomorrow, and leave a much more manageable forty-five miles to finish the following day. Plan C was the most appealing, given our physical and emotional exhaustion, but it also required pushing the polar bear limits a bit. Though Plan B was a good middle ground, we couldn't risk being unable to complete the sixty miles to York Factory before sundown the next day, as paddling in arctic coastal waters in the dark was something we were unwilling to do. Plan A would be the safest from polar bears, but the prospect of paddling through the night in these conditions made me sick. I estimated our chances of surviving to see the sun rise at fifty percent, as our soaking bodies were already pushing the limits of hypothermia. Our spring rain gear was proving to be highly insufficient in the subarctic winter. Grudgingly, we concluded that spending the night here on the clay bank, where our canoe was already parked, was the smart move.

Walking on the steep clay riverbank was a difficult task, especially devoid of any feeling in our toes, or for that matter, any part of our bodies. This location was far from ideal. As we carried the remnants of our moose carcass down the shore and away from camp, we noted the severe angle at which the frozen bank lay.

"We're going to wake up in a ball at the bottom of the tent if we camp here," I said, partially laughing.

"At least we'll be warmer then."

Back at the canoe, as Colton dug through the food pack, I examined the shore further, looking for a spot that was remotely level. Walking away from the canoe in the opposite direction from the moose head, I began to notice that the ground was covered in small, patterned indents. Upon closer examination, I diagnosed the "indents" as wolf tracks, an entire pack's worth of wolf tracks at that. They were much fresher than I would have liked.

"Colton," I called over to him, "we may want to consider a different spot to sleep."

"Oh, calm down. We'll be fine," he said back. "No matter where we go, there's gonna be a bad angle like this." He was still under the impression that I was upset about the sharp incline of the shore.

"No, come over here and check this out, you bonehead," I yelled, pointing to the ground in front of me. If it were up to me, I would have preferred a cliff in exchange for a wolf-less night.

Walking in a slow, deliberate manner, which irritated me more than it should have, he made his way over to observe my discovery.

"Well, crap," he said.

For several seconds, we stood in silence and stared at the tracks, hands on hips, bundled in raingear up to our eyes. We scanned the area and pretended to actually consider moving to a different spot. Of course, we knew all along that we would never pack back up and move. When your mind is set on camping, especially after sixteen straight hours of paddling, nothing is going to change it.

While lying in the soaking wet tent, inside of our soaking wet sleeping bags, and wearing our soaking wet clothes, we still found time for humor. I had finally let the idea of the wolf tracks leave my mind and was drifting into a euphoric dream-state where warmth filled the land. Colton turned over from writing in his journal and gave me a nudge.

"Well, since we're basically out of the bear spray now, if the wolves do come back, we can spray what's left of it on ourselves. That way, we'll at least taste bad," said Colton.

Through chokes of laughter, I managed to sputter out, "Epic voyage."

Words cannot describe the way I felt in the morning. I have never been so cold. We had two days left, and that was an eternity. Lying in the tent, soaked to the core and frozen to the ground, I glared at the icicles that had formed from condensation on the tent walls over my head. If we were miserable now, getting out of the tent and re-entering the windy tundra would be unimaginable. To make matters worse, we were out of pre-cooked meals, leaving our only breakfast option at pancakes cooked with bear spray doused supplies.

Never in my life had I wanted to quit something so completely. To my very core, there was nothing that I wished for more. I didn't know how I would complain about a single inconvenience again for the rest of my life. When and if we would ever get home, I knew that any discomfort would be tolerable. It had to be, because nothing could ever compare to this. How embarrassing that we once complained about chores and homework, or that we felt worry in high school romances and drama. Those issues were nothing. Survival, warmth, a dry bed; those were all that mattered.

In truth, though, there was no way we could quit, and both of us knew it. Even if we could psychologically get over the fact that we had come so far just to end seventy-five miles short, it wasn't physically possible to bow out. Requesting an emergency evacuation would no longer work, and paddling back upstream through the rapids section would take far longer than what we had remaining ahead.

Eventually, I convinced myself to get out of the tent and motivate. Onward was the only option. As I waited for Colton to join me outside, I set up the cooking gear, which was typically his job. I trudged over to the tent and slapped it. Nothing; he was still asleep.

"Get up!" I demanded.

While cooking our pancakes, finally awake, Colton looked at me with a half-smile. "I blame you for this."

I wasn't sure what he meant. "For what?"

"For convincing me to take this stupid trip!"

I smiled for the first time all morning. "Hey," I said. "I just read the book and showed it to you. You're the one who forced us to do those practice trips. If we hadn't, this whole thing wouldn't have happened."

"Okay, we'll agree to disagree," said Colton, taking his first bite of plain pancake. "Oh yes, lovely. The tinge of bear spray actually kind of warms you up. I think I might use it in my cooking at home." He must have been losing it more than I thought.

The first fifteen minutes of paddling were the worst. Our entire bodies, besides our eyes, were covered just like the day before, but it wasn't enough. The excruciating cold was inescapable. In my head, I counted down the minutes before my extremities would go numb, just so they wouldn't feel cold anymore.

At the God's River confluence, sixty miles from York Factory, we pulled over for lunch. This was the location of Sevareid and Port's final campsite, described in their book for its exceptional beauty. Perhaps the weather put a damper on it, but seventy-eight years later and the spot was nothing but a grown in, windy disaster. In my head, I had imagined the confluence of two lazy rivers, meandering kindly towards the bay through a pristine pine forest. Reality painted a far different picture. Prior to converging, each river stretched hundreds of yards wide, and above the tall banks was sparse shrubbery and a swampy forest floor. The sky, land, and water all wore slightly different shades of grey.

Between the rivers, we found only tall weeds along shore, reaching ten feet high, but no trees. We pushed through the thick brush in an attempt to escape the wind, hopeful that the famous campsite was tucked away somewhere, but it was to no avail. Instead of cooking, we saved time by eating a granola bar each. My numb hands lacked the dexterity to take off my gloves, so I resorted instead to pulling them off with my teeth. While chomping down, I deliriously wondered what the hard thing was that I was biting inside my glove. It took several moments to realize that it was my own hand. I attempted to make light of the situation, but neither of us could muster a laugh.

Three miles beyond the God's River confluence, the river now nearly half a mile across, we spotted a white shack on the top of the hundred-foot bank to the right. We pulled over and hiked up the barren hill to investigate. Walking inside, the silence soothed my eardrums after days of constant wind. The shack was a single room, stretching a maximum of fifteen feet across each way. In one corner sat an empty metal stove, connected to a pipe leading through the ceiling. Attached to the far wall were two wooden cots, and it took all of our might to avoid setting out our sleeping bags and calling it a night. We weren't quite far enough to ensure that we would reach Hudson Bay the following day.

It took a minute to realize, but the interior walls of the shack were covered in hundreds of short notes written in marker or pen. The messages dated back dozens of years, and generally included their authors' names, dates, journey, and reason for stopping in. A vast majority of the occupants appeared to be stranded due to inclement weather. Some for days on end. I wondered if their weather was as bad as ours.

As we sat reading other's stories, the low rumble of an engine began to creep within range.

"Plane?" said Colton, peering out the window facing the river and looking to the sky.

"There wouldn't be a plane here," I said, walking out of the shack to catch a better glimpse.

As the noise increased, I realized that it was not coming from above, but from the river below. Three boats, filled to the top of their gunwales with gear, coming from the direction of York Factory, motored up to shore and landed squarely next to our canoe. All seven of the passengers looked up at us in astonishment.

"What are you doing out here in a canoe this time of year?" one called up.

"Trying to get to York Factory!" Colton yelled back. They began climbing up the massive bank and we waited until they reached the top to continue our conversation. The wind made it nearly impossible to hear.

Two of the men were white, from the Canadian military, and the other five were Cree, ranger trainees. They were going to be spending the night in the shack and invited us in to talk. Once inside, several of the Cree men immediately started a fire in the small stove.

"How old are you two anyhow?" one of the military-men asked once he saw our faces inside.

"Eighteen," I responded.

"Jesus," he said. "Why aren't you home with your friends, livin' your life somewhere? This is no place for kids. I thought you were at least in your thirties."

We didn't know what to say. Our modest facial hair and weathered faces must have aged us substantially, but we took exception to his assumption that we were kids, in over our heads.

It turned out that the crew had indeed come from York Factory where they had spent the last several days training. Strangely, one of the military men's last name was Colton. He gave us the bad news that the fort was currently closed. The late winter had delayed the groundskeeper from arriving, and he was the only permanent resident during summer months.

"We know we can't camp there because of the bears, so what should we do if nobody's around?" we asked, alarmed.

"There's a shed behind the keeper's home that should be open. I'd set up camp in there," said Military Colton. "At the very least, there's an outhouse without doors that'll provide some protection from bears and the elements." I prayed that the shed was open.

We chatted for another thirty minutes, justifying the extra break as time that we skipped during our abbreviated lunch. After taking our picture while we prepared for departure, the men informed us of another shack, not as nice as this one, down the river another ten miles. We thanked them and went on our way.

Perhaps the shack they mentioned, or possibly a structure completely different, we found a three-walled hut roughly ten miles later at the top of the east bank. It was primitively built, with cracks in the seams between walls and ceiling, but it provided shelter from the wind and sleet, and it wasn't our wet tent. Inside, the floor was a wooden slab and the walls had no windows. The open side faced the river, which was the source of any type of wind. I wondered who the genius was that set up a three-walled shack in a land where four was necessary. We set down our sleeping bags on the floor and searched the area for wood that might be dry enough to start a fire.

Instead of dry wood, we found something better. A large plastic wall, of a material similar to the walls of a porta-potty, rested against the back of the shed. Pulling the piece around to the open-air front, we tied it up with spare rope, creating a nearly full fourth wall. It wouldn't likely dissuade a polar bear, but at least the wind was eliminated.

The only other valuable resources found outside were an array of tin cans, most rusting away after many winters in the snow. We brought the cleanest-looking can inside to use as a makeshift fire pit by filling it full with some of our white gas.

Huddled around the tin-can fire and cooking a massive portion of rice, we joked about our newfound luxury. Through the cracks in the siding, we could see it was still light out when we finally retired for the evening around midnight. Our alarm was set for 3:30 AM. Sleep could wait until York Factory.

For the first time since before Oxford House, we woke up in full darkness. It didn't last long, but even this far north in June, 3:30 AM looked like a typical night. We scrambled around the floor of our shack, searching with the flashlight for the raingear we had hung up to dry only hours previous. Foggy breath wafted, hardly noticeable in the dark, before our eyes. Locating the gear, we dressed in silence, nervous but thrilled for the hours ahead of us. Forty-five miles away sat the salinized water of Hudson Bay.

Thirty minutes after wake-up, by the time we were packed and ready to leave our final camp of the trip, a dull light had emerged, illuminating one of the most depressing and formidable environments on Earth. The wind and sleet hadn't subsided overnight, and if anything, had strengthened in power. A thick bay fog continued to conceal the whole of the river valley.

After making the switch at God's River the day previous, I was now in the back of the canoe, forcing my eyes to be exposed to the elements just enough to steer. For most of the morning, I kept my eyes closed, understanding full well that Colton had gone through the same pain the day before. Every few seconds, I would reopen them to correct our boat's course. Now heading almost straight north, we bucked the gusting winds that did their best to negate any advantage the current provided. The headwind and current continued to turn against each other, creating angry whitecaps that sprayed water into our canoe and bobbed us up and down like the rollers of Lake Winnipeg.

The view from the slit of my hood and zipped up jacket was wild. Shorelines, still nearly one hundred feet above the river, were bare and brown with the exception of snowbanks, which were becoming increasingly frequent. Each stroke of the paddle pushed us deeper north into polar bear country, and my heart began to race as I half-expected to find one swimming towards our boat around each bend. Their ability to smell other animals is uncanny, and food is scarce near Hudson Bay. The chances of them traveling inland was far from small, especially given the scented moose rack resting atop our outfit. Without our bear spray, there was little we could do if one decided to hunt us down.

Eventually, the severe headwind slowed us to a halt. For fifteen minutes, we paddled in place, trying desperately to avoid the inevitable. How much longer could we go in these conditions, wasting our energy with no progress? When faced with this dilemma previously, it was easy for us to pull ashore and rest. Now, roughly twenty miles from Hudson Bay, stopping on shore was a game of Russian Roulette.

"Aaargh!" I finally yelled, hurling my paddle to the canoe floor. "I can't do it anymore!"

Colton turned around slowly, knowing full well what we had to do. We looked at the shore and watched our hard-fought progress disappear. Every second we neglected our paddles lost us hard fought ground. He nodded and motioned to shore. I picked up my oar in disgust, and we made our way over.

On the open riverbank, we pulled the canoe all of the way out of the water, stretching up towards the flat marshland above. Simultaneously, we crouched together on the leeward side of the vessel. I began to shiver uncontrollably, and my fingers lacked the strength to grasp the tab on the pocket-zipper of my coat. I was attempting to pull out our map, but my fingers couldn't manage it. Giving up with a sigh, I rested my head against the canoe wall.

"This place is death," said Colton, staring blankly forward.

"Maybe we *were* in over our heads," I said, teeth chattering.

"Maybe," said Colton. "I really thought we could do it."

"Me too." His real response to my rhetorical question was the first outward expression of doubt between us. 2,180 miles. Twenty miles short. That was it. A few hours.

"How long do we have here before the polar bears find us?" I asked, my tone somewhere between sarcastic and futile. "Before or after hypothermia sets in?"

"Probably after."

The conversation was becoming too real. My shivering increased, and I began to feel that my mind was lagging two seconds behind reality. Thoughts were slowing down.

"Shame, would've been quite the thrilling way to go out." I sat in silence for a moment. "What do you say we set off the SPOT, just in case? I know they said it would take a couple of days to get to us, but I don't know what other option we have."

I remembered our friends and family back home. They knew we were close but had no idea of our current condition. Setting off the emergency button would send them into a panic.

"Good idea," Colton responded. I wasn't sure if he was serious or not until I watched as he turned to reach into our emergency pack, resting inside the canoe at the feet of the stern position. "May as well see if the emergency button will work."

I stared at the SPOT Messenger emerge from the pack and watched Colton hold the "on" button down. A red light flashed consistently beneath the power button (we never had switched out the dying batteries), and Colton's thumb shifted slowly to the "Emergency" button on the other side. An extra ridge surrounded the button, preventing an accidental push. It looked to me like a reminder that this feature was a last resort. We had never pushed it, and frankly, we didn't know what it did. Maybe the Mounties were wrong, and rescue would be on its way instantly. I wanted nothing more than to be released from the pain right here and now.

Resting his finger atop the button, I waited for him to push it down. This would be our end, and the suffering would go away. At this point, I wasn't sure if that release would be through rescue or through death, but sitting in the subarctic tundra, I hardly cared anymore. No more cold, no more pain, no more hunger. That was all that mattered. After half a minute, he still hadn't pushed it.

"What're you waiting for?" I asked finally.

He looked at me, eyes wide. "I can't."

"What do you mean?"

"I mean I can't!" Colton moved his finger back to the power button and held it down. The red light ceased its flashing, and he stuffed the device back into its pack. "We can't give up."

He wasn't making any sense. The cold had clouded my mind, and his words processed too slowly through my brain.

"Hudson Bay or Bust, man," he said. "We're not going to quit on shore. We're going to see York Factory or die trying. If we fail, we're gonna fail on the water."

"But how? You were out there; the wind is too strong. We can't move forward."

"We have to find a way," he said bluntly. "I refuse to quit."

I was brought back to the first week. Colton had been miserable.

Stomach flu, homesickness, and the onset of tendonitis plagued him, and he wanted to quit. More than anything, he wanted to quit. But he didn't. For whatever reason, he stuck with it, and now we were here, tasked with the same two options. He hadn't quit on me then, and I wasn't going to quit on him now.

I looked him in the eyes. He had the glow of confidence that I had only seen when he was certain something could be done. It was the same look he had when suggesting our practice run down the St. Croix River years before... the practice trip that sparked everything. I knew by this look that we could do it.

"Okay," I said. "Let's do it."

We grasped hands and helped each other up. Something in us had changed, and I felt enough energy within to do anything. Back out into the windy Hayes, we pushed ourselves to a new extreme, forcing our canoe to continue onward.

Fifteen miles from York Factory, the river, though still wide, split into channels that surrounded small islands and which grew dangerously shallow over sand and gravel bars. The river began turning northeast, and the added land cover provided enough wind protection to ease our paddling. Progress began to accelerate, and the added movement finally warmed our bodies.

Our progress slowed again ten miles from Hudson Bay. The wind protection was no different, though it seemed the banks were gradually petering down, dropping toward sea level. It occurred to us that we were perhaps experiencing the first sign of approaching the ocean: a rising tide. The smell of salt began to fill the air too, so we knew we were close. I didn't want to let my guard down, but I was beginning to believe once again that we could do this. We just had to keep pushing.

After passing Fishing Island, five miles upstream from the bay, my grip on the paddle's handle clenched in anticipation at every corner, expecting it to be our last. The channels had carried us to the right side of the river, and we knew that at any moment a gap at the end of the channel-ways would appear in the distance, the land receding into the water. It wouldn't come without a fight. The Hayes demanded more and more effort. We were back on the Minnesota

River, fighting the tireless force against us with every ounce of energy we could muster. It was the Hayes River's last attempt to contain us, its last attempt to even the score.

Finally, it came.

CHAPTER 16

Through the Fog

It was tough to tell because of the thick fog, but we knew what we were looking at. Up ahead, at the very tip of the horizon where the white sky met the grey river, we saw it. Hudson Bay. We were there. Through spring floods, fighting the current, torrential rain and wind, merciless mud, insanity on Lake Winnipeg, raging whitewater, the re-emergence of winter, and near-hypothermic death, we were there. Somewhere on the left bank, only a few miles away, was York Factory.

Colton dropped his paddle to his feet and put his hands on his head. I whooped and hollered in delighted shock. Super Bowl champions didn't feel this accomplished. Pulling out our disposable camera, I captured our view. It didn't look like much, but we knew the true significance.

"I can't believe it," I said.

Colton reached back and I forward, to grasp arms in a numb handshake. Tears of joy, pride, and relief flowed down our dirty cheeks.

"Let's get there," said Colton. "There's a couple of victory cigars with our names on 'em."

We pushed ahead with our goal, York Factory, in sight. At least, the spot where we believed York Factory to be was in sight. The tide was only growing stronger, and we first had to cross over the sandbars that separated us from the left-most channel of the river, knowing that was where we would find the old fort. Shore was now only about thirty feet tall, but so steep that we had no chance of climbing up the mud bank without a rope or steps. On top of the bank, both the trees and snow grew denser. We peeled our eyes for a glimpse of a white building or flag, waiting for any man-made structure at all to peek through the trees.

I thought for a moment about the abundance of snow on shore and concluded that Hudson Bay was likely still frozen over. Usually, June was prime time for the bay to lose its ice, especially with the polar caps vastly receding in recent years. During the annual ice-out was when polar bears would hop off of their melting homes and swim to shore, searching for any form of live meat. Before the melt, the bears rarely venture inland. Still, I thought our wretched scent might kick off their annual migration early.

Just as I was about to suggest pulling over to check the map in case something had gone wrong, we saw a pole sticking out over the short pines above the bank. A Canadian flag blew in the wind at its top. We screamed and shouted in elation as we approached a wooden staircase that led up the shore. The bottom of the stairs rested twenty gently sloped feet from shore, which was littered with logs and, shockingly, moose antlers. It turned out we were not the only ones to collect a souvenir en route to Hudson Bay. I didn't have time, though, to wonder why so many remained on shore; a celebration was in order!

We jumped out of the canoe and onto the sticky clay. Sinking down a few inches, we hopped toward each other for another handshake and embracing hug.

"I love and hate you, man," said Colton with a grin.

"I just hate you," I said jokingly, sitting back down on the canoe to support my weak knees.

Unlike our departure, there was no group waiting for us at the landing. No welcoming committee to greet us at York Factory. But that was fitting, really. We appreciated our family and friends for seeing us off, but through it all, it made sense for Colton and me to share the moment with only each other. The silence after our brief celebration was representative of the adventure as a whole.

Ten feet of boardwalk stretched out from the bottom of the stairs, where we set our gear before pulling the canoe up as far as we could, tying it loosely to a tree at the top of the bank. With the coming tide, we had no idea how high the water levels would rise.

At the top of the stairs, we looked out onto a massive clearing. About one thousand feet along shore and five hundred feet deep into land, the clearing sat upon a marsh-like grassland that would clearly struggle to support our meager weight. To compensate for the soft ground, wooden boardwalks stretched around the land, connecting the bundle of buildings straight ahead to a prominent white structure in the opposite corner. We knew the white structure to be the historic trading post, with windows neatly placed equally across its second floor. On top was a shallow grey roof. Hundreds of years of history sat across from us.

Directly in front of us, ensuring that no visitor would miss it, a sign read "No Camping. Beware Black and Polar Bears." Passing the sign in understanding, we walked to the cluster of buildings straight ahead. One, the most prominent, was the groundskeeper's home, which looked relatively modern. Around it were several small shacks and a doorless outhouse.

Remembering what the Canadian military men had told us the night before, we attempted anyway to locate human life inside the keeper's house. The steps leading up to the three different doors all had boards with nails jutting upwards, pounded through from the other side, we assumed to deter bears from climbing up. Tiptoeing around them, we knocked for several minutes, peering through the windows and wondering how it was possible for it to look so inhabited. Books lay open on the desks and food was sitting out. Perhaps the rangers in training stayed here and forgot to clean up.

After circumnavigating the house several times, we stopped on the wind-protected side, set the SPOT Messenger on the boardwalk and ignited its signal. This time was for real, and it would let our parents know we had made it. There was no way to tell if they received the message or when the floatplane that we ordered would come. It was 2:00 PM, and all that was left to do was wait.

Crouched beside the house, we began to shiver again. The initial excitement of successful arrival had worn off, and standing still allowed the cold to catch back up.

"What do you say we find that shed those guys mentioned might be open?" I said. My voice tinged with slight desperation at the reality that our travels were no longer within our control.

The first building we tried, right behind the house, was locked. Next, I walked over to the outhouse to see if it would suit us as a last resort. Unable to even make it inside due to the scent, uncleaned through a freeze and thaw, I crossed it off the list. Without a door, the outhouse would have done little to deter bears anyhow.

Colton, standing at the door to a silver metal shed on a platform three steps up, pulled at the handle. It opened. Inside was packed with shelves, cooking gear, signs, and even books from wall to wall. We picked our way through the mess to the far side where a desk sat facing a window that looked back towards the keeper's home, and beyond that to the shore of Hudson Bay.

"This'll do," said Colton.

We moved some of the planks with nails in them to the steps of our shed for added security, brought our gear inside, and spread it out to dry. At a minimum, it would likely be a couple of hours before the plane arrived, so it made sense to get comfy.

Finally set, we lit up. The cigars had been purchased way back in Wahpeton, at the start of the Red River. It was only a month ago, but may as well have been a lifetime. I coughed on the stale taste, not being much of a smoker, but powered through regardless. If I could canoe from Minneapolis to Hudson Bay, surely I could finish this tiny cigar.

5:00 PM came and went, and still we had not been picked up. No plane had entered the sky, no person had walked ashore. It was beginning to feel like we had been abandoned. For the last few hours, the two of us had been sitting idly by, waiting for any sign of life to show. The window from our shed provided a decent view of the sky, but in case we missed it, we also watched intently where the boardwalk met the riverbank, waiting for the pilot to appear from below. Before long, Colton and I soon made the disturbing realization that there was no way a floatplane would attempt a landing in seas as awful as this. An optimist would be hopeful for a nicer day tomorrow, but four days in a row of rain or sleet, sub-forty-degree temperatures, and non-stop wind made optimism a luxury impossible for us to imagine. If a plane couldn't arrive in this weather, we naturally assumed it unlikely to arrive for several more days.

We poured a portion of our white gas into a can and lit it, just as we had the night before. In minutes, the entire shed was toasty, and we became uncomfortably hot. Imagine that – hot! Both of us had yet to finish the book we had purchased in Wahpeton, and there was another intriguing enough book found in the shed, so we switched back and forth in reading those.

Eventually, I became antsy, recognizing the fact that our investigation of York Factory lacked serious depth. An exploration of the grounds was in order, and I itched for some excitement. Colton offered to stay behind and watch for the pilot, so I set off on the hike alone.

With a final look at the tin shed behind me, Colton inside, I walked along the boardwalk towards the white fort across the clearing. Approaching it, I noticed that every window and door was boarded up and nailed shut. I wondered if this was always the case, or only when the site was unmanned. Entrance into the historic fort would be impossible without a crowbar and serious motivation, neither of which I possessed at the moment. Looking from the outside sufficed plenty, as breaking and entering was not on my bucket list of York Factory activities. Behind the Fort, tucked even more deeply into the permafrost marsh, was a shack smaller than the one that Colton and I had commandeered. Out of curiosity, I checked the locks, and despite the fact that it was a gust of wind away from complete collapse, I had a glimmer of hope that it would be inhabited. My hopes were dashed by another locked door, so I continued along the boardwalk towards the water.

Back at the shore, now in the opposite corner of the clearing from our storage shed, I noticed that the wooden planks did not, as I had assumed, end. Instead, they veered sharply to the left, and into the dark woods beyond. Without hesitation, I continued on. Two hundred yards into the woods, I came upon another clearing, this one perhaps one-tenth of the size of the field housing the main fort. Lacking a structure of any kind, the clearing held what would have been a gorgeous view of where the river meets the ocean, if not for the dismal weather.

On I went, ignoring the frequent signs that warned pedestrians of polar and black bear dangers in the area. Back into the drenched forest I followed the boardwalk, and yet again it emerged in another small clearing, this one with several broken down homes. At the far end were more signs, all reading the same thing: "Warning! No camping. Use extreme Caution. Beware Polar Bears and Black Bears." This time, I suddenly felt uneasy. My common sense, lagging behind sluggishly from my near-hypothermic morning, had finally caught up to my sense of adventure. Here I was, in the heart of polar bear country, the most notorious "man-hunting" bear in the world, and I was walking alone without even the slightest bit of self-defense. Apparently, my intelligence continued to lag too, as I smiled to myself, then pushed on. There was a sense of deep history in the old structures. I could feel it and didn't want to turn back, knowing that I would likely never get a chance to see this place again.

The slippery boardwalk developed into a staircase running down a hill, still parallel to shore. At the bottom, there was a small stream flowing under the walkway, and immediately afterwards, I was directed right back up the hill, where there were what appeared to be more grown-in ruins of an old village. In the days of the fur trade, a small Cree settlement permanently called this place home. A broken down church was the most prominent figure, sitting directly next to a tiny graveyard, holding no more than fifty tombstones. A faded fence, mostly in shambles, surrounded the graveyard below the foggy backdrop.

I finally became aware of how truly alone I was, and the eerie stillness caused a strong sense of discomfort. Regrettably, I didn't have a camera with me, so I was never able to share the scene. Perhaps this was good, for I don't believe that any picture would do it justice. Without hesitation, I took this opportunity to let my better judgment take hold and turned around, heading back to Colton and safety.

By the time I reached the storage shed, my pace was an all-out sprint. Inside, I found that Colton hadn't moved an inch. He seemed unsurprised with the length of time I was gone and had apparently been engrossed by his reading. I rehashed my adventures with him and decided that they were "had to be there" moments due to his lack of enthusiasm.

It was 6:30 by the time of my return, and still no plane had arrived. The wind had seemingly subsided, but we accepted the fact that we would be spending our night here. As we ate some of our remaining sweets for dinner (we had finished the real food), I thought in silence about how odd it was to be done. There was nowhere to go, no schedule to keep up with, no destination. Our lives had been defined by a destination, and here we were. The not-so-glamorous finish to the trip seemed to leave a residual effect, giving us the feeling that we had not finished at all. No crowd was here to congratulate us, and although we assumed our parents were relieved to see us check in, we remained alone in the tundra. I was neither happy nor sad… or perhaps, I was both.

I woke first the following morning, as usual, on the storage-shed floor. When I looked at the clock, I noticed it read 7:30… sleeping in! The time, though, was not the most noticeable feature to the clock. There was a new, strange number on the temperature display. It was fifty degrees. I jumped up and looked out the window. Sun! Imagine that, the day after we finished and it was fifty degrees with hardly a cloud in the sky; a perfect canoeing day, of course.

Wearing short sleeves and shorts, I stepped outside onto the stairs leading down to the maze of boardwalks. The SPOT messenger lay untouched on the bottom step. With a good deal of hope, I set it off again, reminding our parents that we were ready to go home. Some wind remained, of course, as we were on the shores of the southern Arctic Sea, and the open landscape provided little cover. With the current weather, though, I felt that if a floatplane couldn't pick us up today, it would never be able to. It was the nicest day we had seen in a week, and I didn't imagine we would be blessed with many more like it. We made up our minds that we would set off the SPOT messenger every fifteen minutes, simply to convey the direness of our situation to our parents.

Several hours passed, and still no plane arrived. We began to grow genuinely worried. Our leftover sweets would only tide us over for so long, and then what? Ideas on how to break into the keeper's cabin became more than just an option of casual consideration. It would be simple enough to leave our information behind so that we could pay them back. Of course, we would wait at least another couple of days before going to this measure, but our minds naturally planned for the worst.

At 11:30 AM, we finally heard it, the unmistakable sound of an engine, this time surely not a boat. We ran outside and searched the sky. For several seconds, there was nothing. Then we spotted it, circling York Factory like a bird of prey; the floatplane was investigating its choppy landing zone. Frantically, we waved our arms around, praying that the pilot would notice our aggravated condition and not head home to try again later. After a few more circles, the plane made its way down to the water and landed. Casually, we walked back into our shed and began packing up. Over the last twenty-two hours, we had made it our home, and our gear was strewn about accordingly.

From our front window, we spotted the pilot climb up the steep staircase and onto the boardwalk. Colton walked outside and gave him a cheery wave. We happily anticipated a conversation with somebody other than each other.

"If you're not in my plane in five minutes, I'm leaving without you!" yelled the pilot. He was running, not walking, towards us. Standing dumbfounded, we stared at the man. Shorter than us and sporting a full brown beard that matched the untidy hair on the top of his head, he looked frazzled.

"Huh?" Colton said back, half smiling at the chance that the pilot was joking.

"The tide is going out, and if we're not off the bay SOON, we'll all be stranded here." The pilot, now at the steps of our shed, motioned to his plane with a jerk of his arm.

Without further ado, we crammed everything we thought we owned from the little shed into our packs. It didn't matter if it fit, or if we would tear our bags in haste, we were not going to be left here.

Several items, including my rain pants, were accidentally left behind in the rush.

In a time apparently close enough to five minutes, we were back at the riverbank with our gear in hand. The plane was parked some one hundred yards down the mucky shore from our canoe, forcing us to paddle for the last time of the trip. It felt strange to paddle again. Just less than a day removed from the water and we were already losing our canoeing muscles. Once to the plane, the pilot assisted us in aggressively throwing our luggage on board. Saving the best for last, we attempted to include the moose antlers on the heap of things to pack.

"Nope. That can't come on," said the pilot firmly.

Colton made a face that hinted towards argument.

"It'll take me months to get that smell outta here. It's already gonna take a few weeks from the smell of you two! Plus, customs won't let you bring that thing outta the country anyhow."

Slightly insulted at his jab at our personal hygiene, however true it was, we understood that we were in no position to argue. After all, he *was* the man that would be delivering us back to civilization. The mystery of the dozens of deer and moose antlers scattered about shore was solved. It appeared that we were not the only sorry individuals to be denied.

Upon fastening our canoe onto the left float of the seaplane, the pilot wasted no time. Colton in the back with our packs, and me in the "copilot" position (I didn't dare ask for any responsibilities), we taxied away from shore and into the uncomfortably choppy bay. Never having ridden in a floatplane before, my knuckles were as white as chalk, squeezing the handles during the rocky take off. We rode the waves up and down, seemingly gaining little to no speed, and surely not enough to become airborne. I glanced over, attempting to decipher our pilot's face, waiting for any sign of panic. Then, in an instant, the rough bouncing became smooth, and I could almost feel the air beneath my feet, between the plane's floats and the water.

Straight ahead, a dense blue sky covered my field of vision as the plane's nose aimed upward. For nearly a minute, we continued to climb before finally leveling out. The view was shocking – the Hayes

River emptied into a vast sea, open water for perhaps five miles, and then an endless cover of white. This had been our goal, our end destination, for much more than the last fifty days. We had been working towards this view for five years, over a quarter of our lives, and here it was, the ice-covered arctic sea: Hudson Bay.

Our pilot, much friendlier after take-off, humored Colton and me by twice circling York Factory, presenting us with views of our home for the previous day.

After allowing us time to snap a few pictures, the pilot turned his compass bearing west and slightly south, towards the town of Gillam. For fifteen minutes, we followed along the Hayes River, retracing our paddle strokes at a speed that made our four miles per hour downright laughable. Nonetheless, the view of this god-forsaken river from several thousand feet above created a nostalgia I didn't expect. Granted, it was a sunny and clear day, but the river and land below seemed so peaceful from up here. Already, less than a full day after the misery of the Hayes, I found it difficult to remember exactly how life on the river had truly felt. Colton sat behind me, wedged between our packs, eating the last of his fruit snacks and granola bars that he had so diligently rationed during the more trying moments of the trip. I smiled in disbelief. We were going home.

CHAPTER 17

Re-entry

"What will your next trip be?"

The question came from the third row, a middle-aged woman with brown bangs, glasses, and an inquisitive smile. She looked excited, inspired even, to hear our response. The rest of the crowd around her murmured in agreement. They all wanted to know.

I looked beyond the woman. A few hundred people were packed into the back conference hall at an REI outdoors store in Bloomington, a suburb of Minneapolis twenty miles from Chaska. The event had been advertised in the regional newspapers, but we hadn't expected the standing-room-only crowd. In the back were two news crews from different stations. Sitting in a row of chairs to the right, our families and Nick Coleman watched with proud smiles.

We had just finished going through a slideshow of pictures from the trip. Less than a week prior, our floatplane had landed in Gillam, Manitoba after the short ride from York Factory. Each day, the distance from us to the experience grew exponentially, so telling stories to this crowd brought us back in a way. They laughed about our run-in with the freight train near Ortonville where Colton had thought we died. They cheered when we cursed the Red River mud and treeless North Dakota plains. They even shook their heads in astonishment when we convinced them that bear-spray-flavored pancakes really are satisfying when you're frozen to your very core.

I looked at Colton, waiting for him to answer the question about our next plans. In truth, we weren't sure. We had toyed with the idea of attempting to complete the fastest paddle down the Mississippi River, or taking a shot at the Yukon River one-thousand-kilometer race. Both would require a hefty investment in a racing canoe, though, and neither would involve much sleep or enjoyment of nature. Perhaps a bit lazy, I was always more partial to the nature aspect.

"We think we'll do the Yukon 1000," Colton finally answered. "We'll have to figure some things out first, though."

"What was the hardest part?" asked an elderly man from the back.

"All of it," I said immediately, to a room full of laughter. I wasn't joking but figured that a more specific answer was in order. "The first week and the last, I would say. The first was tough physically, paddling upstream and allowing our muscles to adapt to canoeing all day. The last was a mental challenge. At one point, I honestly wasn't sure we would make it." That was the most I wanted to share about our most trying moments on the final day. I was about to mention how close we were to failing... to quitting or dying only miles from Hudson Bay. But, for the same reason that we hadn't disclosed the moment of weakness to the *Star Tribune* in the first story after we finished, I kept it secret. Frankly, we were ashamed. Embarrassment was a silly emotion, we knew, since in the end, we never did give up. We finished.

"I've never been so miserable."

"Or proud," yelled another member of the audience, quoting one of Mr. Coleman's final articles about us. The rest of the crowd applauded.

"Why did you do it?" piped up a young boy in the front row, his eyes wide with interest. He reminded me of the sophomore from Ms. Flom's class that had asked me the same question earlier that year. Their tones, though, were opposite.

"To prove that we could," said Colton. "And not just that we could. But that anybody could. We wanted to prove that adventure isn't lost in today's world. You just really need to *want* it."

I nodded. "People think adventure is gone. It's not. Everybody craves it in some form, even if it's not in the wilderness. We found our adventure by retracing Sevareid and Port, but anybody can find an adventure meaningful to them." I paused for a moment, considering my next words. "It's not so much *where* you go, but it's that you *do* go. Never be afraid to follow your dreams."

Driving back to Chaska from REI in Colton's 1986 Chevy, the two of us sat in silence. We were used to it. From Gillam, a town of 1200 people, we took a twelve-hour bus ride back to Winnipeg the day after arriving. A bus ride of that length, I venture, would bore most people, but Colton and I sat content for the entire ride, happy with only our thoughts to amuse us. The rapidly changing scenery of a sixty-mile-per-hour vehicle only added to the excitement.

Leaving the presentation in Bloomington took some time, as many people wished to ask one-on-one questions, have us autograph books or paddles, or simply to shake our hands. We conducted a handful of TV and newspaper interviews in the parking lot on our way out.

Home with a couple hours left of daylight, we decided to strap the old Bell North Bay to the bed of Colton's truck, to take her for a spin. The North Bay had fared us well during the first half of the trip, and there was always a twinge of guilt that we didn't ride her all the way to the bay, even though it might have cost us our lives. We decided to honor her now.

Down to the Minnesota River, at the very park where we set off in late April, we pushed off into calm water. No longer in flood stage, the river was substantially lower and slower than when we began. It would have been an absolute joy to paddle up the Minnesota like this!

Empty, the North Bay was far tippier than what we were used to with the Bell Alaskan. Unable to ride atop the bus on our twelve-hour drive back to southern Canada, the Alaskan was picked up by a semi-truck passing through Gillam and dropped off at a warehouse in Winnipeg. With my father, who met us at the Winnipeg bus station, we picked up our faithful canoe for the remaining car ride home.

After finishing high school back in March, we one day pushed off into the river just like today, with nothing but a rock to weigh down the canoe for ballast. It had been our first attempt at practicing the Minnesota River current, and we, for some reason, decided to switch positions in the canoe, from stern to bow, in the middle of the river. Somebody from the nearby highway must have seen us, for a police officer was waiting at the landing when we arrived back. He didn't believe we were eighteen, or seniors who had graduated early, so he phoned the school to ensure our story checked out.

Now in late June, only three months later, nobody questioned our age. My unkempt beard remained from the trip, though I had tidied my hair slightly. Colton was clean shaven enough to resemble the day of our departure. Appearance-wise, we were hardly older than on April 28th, but there was no doubt that we had changed. Re-entry back into civilization was not an instant or easy process. We each had lingering numbness in our fingers and toes from the constant cold, and mattresses remained unnatural. It took time to accept that food and comforts could be obtained in an instant, and that people took this for granted. Friends mentioned how it seemed that although we were physically present, our minds were miles away, somewhere in the Canadian bush, surviving. We were technically home, but it wasn't the same as we had left it. Things had changed; we had changed.

Acclimating to the North Bay didn't take long. She had been our home for a month, and that bond had not been lost. We paddled upriver to the first bend. Here, our friends had thrown rocks at us and we had joked about hiding a motor. One reporter, days after arriving home, asked us jokingly what kind of motor we used. Our response: weather too cold to sit still.

We sat at the bend for some time, joking and reminiscing about the last two months of our lives. It was always obvious that years from now, we would look back and realize how crazy we were, but we already knew it. As absurd and miserable as we were however, Nick Coleman was right. More than anything, we were proud.

The experience taught us about life, about friendship and brotherhood, the generosity and greatness of humankind, about connecting with nature, and appreciating the luxury of modern society. It taught us that nothing in life worth having or doing comes easy, and that if we really wanted to, we could accomplish any dream. Above all else, though, it taught us that adventure can be found right out your own back door, and it can take you anywhere.

"Epic voyage," said Colton.

"Yeah, it was," I replied. "Let's go find another one."

Acknowledgements

As proud as we were to fulfill our dreams and paddle a canoe from the Twin Cities to Hudson Bay, it would be folly to say that Colton and I accomplished this task entirely on our own. Yes, we used our own arms and muscles to power the canoe, but the help and kindness of strangers along the way was both beneficial toward the ultimate goal, and an enhancement of the experience as a whole. We would like to take this time to acknowledge a few of those who were influential in our success:

- Dan and Kathy Witte for their tremendous support before, during, and after the completion of our adventure. Kathy also was the creator of our website, and maintained it along the way to provide progress reports, update media stories, and manage donations.
- Patrick and Patricia Bloomfield for, despite our reckless ambitions, supporting our ideas whether they were successful or not. Thank you for, with Dan and Kathy Witte, meeting us on our layover days and re-supplying our pre-cooked chicken packets, new canoe, and the makeshift spray skirt.
- Nick Coleman for the keen interest in our adventure, and for kicking off the publicity that spurred interest in us along the way.
- Nancy Flom for opening up her classroom to spread the word of our adventure to underclassmen at Chaska High School.
- Bruce from the Belle Plaine landing for inspiring us with his stories of adversity and exploration no matter what life brought his way.
- Bert Ackerman for taking aerial photographs and meeting us for lunch in Le Sueur.
- Jim and Ginny for their hospitality, two days in a row, at Turner Hall in New Ulm.
- Jason and Jane from the Milan Beach Resort for taking us in during the weather layover on Lac Qui Parle, and treating us to dinner. Jane asked only for a postcard from York Factory in return, which unfortunately did not exist, so hopefully this acknowledgement will be a successful replacement.
- The Johnson family in Fargo, who made the most memorable home cooked meal of the journey, and graciously drove us into

town for additional supplies.

- Diny Houle and the Houle family for allowing us to store our canoe in the shed of their Letellier farm. The bridge over the river near their land was rebuilt, and in the process of construction their farm torn down. It is with our sincerest hope that the Houle family is in good spirits, despite a new location for their abode.
- David in Winnipeg for providing us a safe place to sleep in the Winnipeg city limits, and for sharing travel stories into the night.
- David and Erik from Norway House, who showed us the way of the Cree along the Echimamish River. Their guidance and companionship was greatly appreciated.

In writing, editing, and publishing *Adventure North*, a variety of people helped turn words on a page into a fully-fledged novel. Of course, Colton Witte was not only instrumental in the adventure itself, but in the editing, publishing, and marketing of *Adventure North*. Beth Hercules provided a phenomenal round of copyediting, and then proofreading. Beth also formatted the book for print and e-edition. Grant Herschberger, Patricia Bloomfield, and Dan Witte all beta read, and edited the novel, providing tremendous assistance. Katie Olson was a fabulous consultant for printing the book, and Randy Herget designed the perfect cover to exemplify our adventure.

Throughout the years that it took to write this story, the support that I received from my loving wife, Sarah, was second to none. Through busy schedules, Sarah always respected my "writing time," and understood the level of work that authoring and publishing this story would take. Without her backing, none of this would have been possible.

Finally, I would like to give my sincerest thanks to those who pre-ordered copies of the book. Their support paved the way for publishing *Adventure North*. Additionally, Tom Stauber deserves great thanks. He followed our trip from the start, and upon hearing about the book, Tom pre-ordered 100 copies, which helped the publishing process immensely. Thank you to the following:

Mary and Greg LePage	Lola Sibcy
Santa Williamson	John Kreutzberger
Karen Bouton	Ross and Cori Eichelberger

Betsy and Nate Witte
Mary Register
Kent Dickinson
Lory Keranen
Tonye Hosch
Tom and Karen Stauber
Nancy Johnson
Scott and Susan Mitchell
David and Brende Witte
Eleta Donaldson
Jeff and Jean Witte
Matt Ellingson
Paul Bradach
Tyler and Jennifer Witte
Tim and Heidi Gerten
John and Betty Sjovall
Sharon and Steve Herron
Courtney McDougal
Julie Buckles
Thomas Lapka
Elsa Kendall
Travis McKee
Maggie Goshert
Hannah Kneeland
Anna Stauber
Dwayne and Julie Johnson
Dave Vancura

Steve and Victoria Hosch
Donna and Gerry Witte
Sherry LePage
Lynda Priebe
Tom and Nancy Bloomfield
Patrick and Patricia Bloomfield
Lisa Gearman
Jim Vangerud
Sam and Shannon Ebenreiter
Joseph Chu
Taylor and Tyler Trabant
Erik Doeden
Barbara Forbrook
Ann Berkhof
Jeremy Wittrock
Carol Scheffler
Ken and Kayla Hanus
Kathy Tracy
Kyle Lamb
Cade Plath
Gary Goeman
Kathy and Danyl Witte
Ann Tracy
Jay Viner
Tony Happ
Emily and Ben Titus
Ali Witte

Sean Bloomfield (Author)

Sean teaches 8th grade social studies and coaches high school hockey in Chaska, MN. After canoeing to Hudson Bay, he attended Minnesota State University, Mankato, where he received both his Bachelors and Masters degrees in Education. In the summer of 2011, he and three college friends (Colton Witte, Blake Spanier, and Sam Ebenreiter) lived off the land in the Absaroka-Beartooth Region of Montana for one month. Sean currently lives in Chaska with his wife and children.

Colton Witte (Creative Editor)

Colton studied international relations, institutional philosophy, and business at Minnesota State University, Mankato. He continues to backpack, canoe, fish, and hunt with friends and family, and enjoys exploring music and culture with his girlfriend. In his free time, he plays guitar and sings, performing professionally in weddings and at social events. Currently, Colton resides in Minneapolis.

Colton and Sean after receiving the new food pack in Judson, MN.

Colton, the chef, hard at work.

Sean eating lunch on the Minnesota River.
The farm in the background nestled directly up to the riverbank.

The Minnesota River spills over the riverbank between Granite Falls and Montevideo.

The first morning of "the shifts."

Too close for comfort...

Bottom of the lock in Lockport, Manitoba.

Netley Lake, Manitoba.

First view of Lake Winnipeg - an inland sea.

...an in the marsh of
...etley Lake.

Layover day on the big water.

Cold Pizza for breakfast after
a night beneath the stars.

Polar bear? Or snowbank?

Warren Landing.

Posing with the Mounties of Norway House.

Painted Stone Portage.

What happens when Colton wins a cracker-toss. Water to the canoe's brim.

The last blue sky of the trip - Knee Lake, Manitoba.

Scouting in the rapids section.

Sean readying breakfast at the wolf track campsite.

Colton's souvenir.

The God's River flowing in from behind on the left, the Hayes River on the right.

The mighty Hayes River, thirty miles from Hudson Bay.

On the horizon: Hudson Bay.

View from the storage shed. Historic fort in the distance.

Welcome Home Party -
Colton with family.

Welcome Home Party -
Sean with family.

Arrival in Gillam, Manitoba